Books by J. Frank Dobie

Apache Gold and Yaqui Silver

Tom Lea

Apache Gold & Yaqui Silver

By J. Frank Dobie · Illustrated by Tom Lea

Boston · Little, Brown and Company · 1950

Fourteenth Printing

THE TRAIL OF A STORY HUNTER

Along in 1927 a newspaper friend told me that the next time I was in El Paso I had better run down a lawyer named Harris Walthall for a good story. Early one morning of the December following I announced myself at Walthall's office. He said he knew a little of the story, but that the man to tell it was a mining engineer named Frank Seward. He took me to Frank Seward. He talked two or three hours, and then he said I must see C. B. Ruggles to get the real details. A little after dark we got out to the house where Ruggles stayed when he happened to be in town, which was seldom. I barely caught a midnight train going up to Socorro, in New Mexico. Nobody but Ruggles had talked, and I could not go to sleep after I got on the train. The story, the story of the long-lost and much-sought-for Tayopa Mine, lost somewhere in the Sierra Madre of Mexico, had me enthralled. About two weeks later I was back in El Paso, on my way east. I telephoned Ruggles, and he came down to the hotel and had supper with me. I barely caught the midnight train to San Antonio. Nobody but Ruggles had talked. He was about to lift out a limitless fortune from the lost mine. Within a month he was going back into the Sierra Madre, where for six years he had been following the trails to Tayopa.

At this time I was writing considerably for the *Country Gentleman* — hunting stories, legendary tales, historical sketches of the old West and Southwest. My trip into New Mexico had been after a panther to put in the *Country Gentleman*. I didn't see one hair out of a panther and the dogs didn't smell one, but Joe and Dub Evans, with whom Paul Bransom — the animal illustrator — and I were hunting, had caught lots of the creatures. They were mighty free with them as we sat around the fire every night. I picked the likeliest-sounding one out of the lot, and it did just as well as if I had run it up a piñon tree myself. When I sent it in, I wrote the editor I had heard the best lost mine story in North America, but would not try to write it without going over the ground. He wired me to roll up my bed and go with Ruggles and find the story whether I found the mine or not. In this book I have told the story with much more incident and background than I told it for the editor who sent me to get its setting. I know a lot more now about Tayopa, the Sierra Madre, and other matters than I knew then. I have an idea that I often know too much for what the average reader regards as good storytelling. I don't think any longer that Tayopa is the great-

The Trail of a Story Hunter

est lost mine tradition in North America; I think the Lost Adams Diggings is.

Not long after I made my first pack trip across the Sierra Madre, Tayopa bound, I began putting into final form my book of tales about lost mines and buried treasures in the Southwest — *Coronado's Children*. At one time I intended to include Tayopa in this, but the limitations of space decided me to leave it for another book — on Mexico. Then I wrote that other book, *Tongues of the Monte* — in some ways the strangest book that has ever been published about Mexico — but the Story of Tayopa, which I had intended to make its foundation, did not fit into it.

Meantime, with pack mule and *mozo*, — the only free way to travel and soak in the country, — frequently lingering on some hacienda, I have gone into and across the Sierra Madre at various places. Never have I been out of the sound of the story of Tayopa. Over a great territory of northern Mexico it is as familiar to Mexican, Indian and gringo, all, as the story of Paul Revere's ride is to American school children. About three years ago a Kentucky distiller offered to take me in his airplane to look for Tayopa a long, long way from where Ruggles thought he had located it. Last year two mining men in Los Angeles with enough money to hire a military guard from President Cardenas of Mexico tried to

[xi]

The Trail of a Story Hunter

persuade my friend Charles A. Newman, of El Paso, to guide them in another direction. A German in Chihuahua City wrote me by air mail to say he had discovered a document that would take any man to the right place. When I saw the document, I understood why it did not take the German to where he suggested it would take me. Leaving out much, I am trying to indicate how Tayopa would not let me rest until I had put it into a book. It may not let me rest now.

Somewhere in *Coronado's Children* I remarked that I really cared about writing the story of one other lost mine — the Adams Diggings. In the summer of 1937 I dug out all the letters inspired by that statement. I had filed them as I received them. Upon examining the aggregate, I was astounded at their bulk and their contents. More people had written to tell me something than to ask help in finding the Diggings. In the Appendix to this book I have given some particulars about these generous people. Into the narrative of the Lost Adams Diggings I have woven some of the characters and experiences met during trips through the mountains of New Mexico trailing down the story.

In order not to be misunderstood, I must admit that my trailing-down of lost mines and buried treasures has been for gold not weighable in avoirdupois scales. How much of an alchemist I am, others must judge. In retelling these stories that were told to me, I have naturally omitted many things, made disconnected parts connect, supplied hinges; but all the essentials are traditional history — or traditional legend.

In *Coronado's Children* I attempted an interpretation of the historical or cultural significance of the traditions of lost mines and buried treasures in America. I care much more, however, about the drama, the flavorsome characters, the vast lands in which the riches lie hidden, the "pictures and conversations" that Alice in Wonderland so approved of, than I care about interpretations. Any authentic record of the lore of a land and a people is, after all, an interpretation. The lore that composes the stuff of this book is, irrespective of the way in which it is presented, a part of one of the deepest and widest epics of North American soil. Phantoms, if you will — but "each shall his favorite phantom pursue." The difference lies not between phantom and non-phantom, but between phantoms themselves.

Two of the stories that follow, "Not the Will of God" and "General Mexhuira's Ghost," are lacking in the historical background characterizing the other narratives. I have included the first because it represents a class of stories common to every mountain in Mexico and to every Mexican's memory and also because it seems to me to reveal the character of the people — good and kindly people nearly always — who live in the country part of Mexico and have no connection with the politicians. For this story I am indebted to my life-long friend Rocky Reagan, rancher in Southwest Texas. So far as I am concerned, anything interesting fits any-where, the quality of being interesting having the right to override the laws of coherence any time. The story of "General Mexhuira's Ghost" interested me extraordi-narily when Charles W. Hackett told it to me, and it interests me even after I have written it. The name of the individual who had the experiences with the ghost has of necessity been disguised. His accounts show per-haps what a man who keeps on following up clues to buried cities, lost mines and the like will eventually come to believe — and make others believe. The setting of this story is far south of, but not foreign to, the Sierra Madre of the North. For the main narrative in "Pedro Loco" I owe my friend Victor Lieb.

"Scalp Hunters' Ledge" and "Not the Will of God" appeared in abbreviated forms in the New York *Herald Tribune Magazine;* one or two short narratives woven into the first section of "The Lost Tayopa Mine" ap-peared in the *Herald Tribune's* successor, *This Week.* As I have already said, the original Tayopa narrative was printed in the *Country Gentleman,* August and Septem-ber, 1928. "Pedro Loco" came out in the *Southwest*

The Trail of a Story Hunter

Review, July, 1938. I thank these magazines for permission to reprint.

I feel a deep appreciation for Maud Durlin Sullivan, Librarian of the El Paso Public Library, and her excellent staff, not only on account of the many helpful courtesies received personally but also on account of the way they have made an institution serve, express and fit the Southwest.

I am grateful to the following for their kind permission to use material from their publications in this volume:

Wilson Erickson, Inc., for an extract from *Black Range Tales* by James A. McKenne.

Houghton Mifflin Company for a long quotation from *Stepsons of Light* by Eugene Manlove Rhodes.

J. Frank Dobie

Austin, Texas
The Comanche Moon, 1938

Contents

[xvii]

The Lost Adams Diggings

THE LOST ADAMS
DIGGINGS

The Lost Adams Diggings is a story of a man and a world.

From the badlands under Huerfano Peak overlooking the San Juan River and the corner made by the states of New Mexico, Arizona, Utah and Colorado, the world stretches southward half a thousand miles across canyon-cut deserts of mesa, through the lava beds called the malpais, into the Datil, the San Mateo, the Mogollon, the Tularosa, the Magdalena, the Black, the Burro and other mountain ranges on down almost to the Mexican border. From east to west the world stretches from the Rio Grande across the great Plains of San Augustine and over mountains and more mountains, the Mimbres River, the forks of the Gila, the ditch-drained San Francisco, the nation-wide lands of the Navajo, the world of the Zuñi and on into Apache fastnesses of Arizona. It is a world of forests and deserts, of great stretches of thirst, of springs, of narrow ribbons of irri-gation-supported population, of mountains without limit and without population of any kind, of silent Indians, of solitudes utterly empty, of a vastness and an aloftness prefiguring for the imagination "the vasty halls of death." It is a world of little rain wherein races of men no longer extant left hieroglyphic records of thriving population, arts, fierce struggle and then vanishment. It is a world of illimitable vistas, of geological inscrutabilities, and of things both animate and inanimate deeply hidden. Man-made highways and automobiles crisscross this world but hardly penetrate it, enter it but scarcely get into it deeper than the furrow of an ocean liner gets into the waters of the everlasting deeps.

Such is the chief actor, the setting itself, in the drama of the Lost Adams Diggings. The man pitted against this protagonist has had many names, diverse features, varying characteristics, but always he has been guided by a single motive, possessed by a single passion, pursuing a single way of life, seeking a single object — gold, the Adams gold, gold found and lost.

I · Enough Gold to Load a Pack Horse

Like Adam, Adams seems to have had no "front name." To the men who hunted with him for the gold he had found and lost, in traditions kept alive by the talk of thousands of people, and in scores of newspaper articles buried by time, he was and is merely Adams of the Diggings, the man himself blotted out by the fabulous lode that for three quarters of a century has kept his name green all over the mining West. Like the names of John Wilkes Booth, Billy the Kid and other notabilities, his has been assumed by impostors, bringing confusion both to his reputation and the plain story he originally told; but he remains the original Adams.

It is known that he was born in Rochester, New York, July 10, 1829, and that in 1861 he began freighting between Los Angeles and Tucson. He was making good money and had learned to talk fair "cowpen Spanish," when along in August of 1864 he delivered a load of freight in Tucson and started back to California. He was alone, his helper having decided to remain in Arizona. He had a team of twelve horses. To his big wagon was attached a trailer, a smaller wagon. Both wagons were empty except that in the jockey box Adams had a few provisions and around two thousand dollars he had collected for freighting.

One evening he camped in the Gila Bend, an oasis that all travelers across the desert from Tucson yearned to reach. He was about twenty miles below the Pima Indian villages. The weather was fine, and after he had hobbled his horses and broiled his salt bacon on a stick, he slept the sleep of the serene. The next morning while he was boiling coffee, he heard yells and hoof-beats. He jumped on a wagon wheel for a view and, looking out over the greasewood, saw five Indians on foot running off his horses, which had grazed some distance away on the flat.

In the frontier manner, he had kept one horse tied at camp. It was saddled. Grabbing his gun and mounting, he took after the thieves. He heard a bullet plunk and saw an Indian stumble. The other four cut the hobbles on two of the horses and, mounted double, set off bareback. Adams was so hot after them, however, that they jumped into a gully and disappeared. The chase and the rounding up of the scattered horses took him more than an hour. Approaching camp, he saw smoke. He galloped ahead to find his wagons burnt beyond rescue, his harness cut to pieces, his provisions gone, his money stolen, and not a marauder in sight. Running off the horses had evidently been a ruse.

All Adams had left was his saddle, gun, and twelve horses. They were not big draft animals, but stout Western horses, saddle-broken, that had been taught to look through a collar. Driving these horses, he now set out for the villages of the friendly Pimas, who were not, he knew, implicated in the attack. Where he had expected to barter for parched corn and dried meat from solitary primitives, he found twenty mining men of his own race with civilized flour and coffee, all highly excited and all astonishingly eager to trade him out of his horses. The cause of their excitement and horse hunger he soon learned. While prospecting near the Pimas, they had struck a faint showing of gold. Among the Indians who saw the color and witnessed the stir over it was a young Mexican man. Unconsciously, he soon turned all interest upon himself. Both in dress and feature, he looked like a "pure quill" Indian. One of his ears was crumpled into a shapeless knot, and from this circumstance he was, as Adams learned, called Gotch Ear.

According to his story, he and a brother had as boys been captured by Apaches on a raid into Sonora. Through years of captivity they grew to be thoroughly Indianized and were regarded by their captors as one of themselves. They did not, however, forget their mother tongue, which various warriors could speak fairly well, and they kept a memory of their homeland. Then something exceedingly rare among Indians occurred — murder. Gotch Ear's brother and a warrior quarreled and the warrior killed the brother. Not waiting for tribal justice, Gotch Ear retaliated on the warrior. Then he fled for his life. He was coursing for his Sonora home. He was afoot and wanted a horse to cross the desert. He had arrived among the Pimas only a day or two before the Americans struck the color of gold.

He was astonished at the excitement. Silver for ornaments he knew. When he saw two fifty-dollar gold pieces belonging to a Californian named Brewer and learned how the metal would buy horses and guns, he was yet more astonished.

"Why," he exclaimed, "I know a canyon in which you might load a horse with this stuff in one day's gathering. There are pieces of it scattered in the gravel as big as acorns. Above the gravel is a rock holding chunks of this yellow stuff as big as a wild turkey's egg."

The miners asked Gotch Ear where this canyon was. He pointed northeast. "In Apacheria," he said, "maybeso ten sleeps. The canyon is *bien escondido* — well hidden."

Then the Americans began trying to induce Gotch Ear to lead them to the gold. The Apaches in whose territory it lay were not those to whom he had been captive, he said, but his captors sometimes mixed with them, and thus it was he had come to enter the canyon. He did not seem to fear the Apaches in that direction. Finally he consented to act a guide for two horses, a saddle, a gun, ammunition, the two fifty-dollar gold pieces, and a red silk bandanna he had spied. To prove his honesty, he agreed that if he could not show what he promised, he would stand up and allow his followers to shoot him. He asked for no advance payment.

But the miners were short on horses, having lost

several to unknown Indian thieves. The Pimas had no horses. The proposed journey was deep into a region where, as the Western saying went, "to be afoot was to be no man at all." Thus affairs stood when Adams rode up with his *caballada*.

Adams had never been interested in mining, had not once gone prospecting. Now the enthusiasm took possession of him. Besides, he felt that he had nothing to lose, having already lost all — all but his horses. On condition that he furnish the twelve animals, two of them to be paid the guide, he was offered the leadership of the expedition. He agreed.

They set out on August the twentieth. Including the guide, there were twenty-two men. They had twelve pack animals. Not a single white man at that time lived in the territory to be traversed. Not a landmark was known by name to any English-speaking man of the expedition. Gotch Ear rode ahead. Adams, as he subsequently demonstrated over and over, had almost no sense of direction and was very poor at retaining in memory any picture of any route he went over. The accounts that he gave years later of the course now followed were all vague and confused.

It lay steadily northeast, with jogs for water, but the time for rains, late summer, had not failed and water was fairly plentiful — if one knew where to find it. Gotch Ear knew. At length he skirted a high mountain, the description of which, but not the location, fits Mount Ord. On a saddle between this and another mountain they made camp.

The next morning before packing up, the guide led Adams and several other men to a summit and, pointing northeast to two peaks that in the far distance looked to be anywhere from one hundred to two hundred miles away, said, "The canyon of the gold is near those peaks. Maybeso in six days we come to the door that goes in."

No Mexican or Indian ever overestimates distance. His only conception of distance is in the time required to traverse it. Twenty-two men, unorganized, unused to traveling together, burdened with pack animals, travel slowly. Adams always claimed that the pack horses were kept in a trot. He was sure that the party skirted the White Mountains of eastern Arizona. He claimed also that after leaving the Gila River they crossed only two streams. In the Land of Little Rain, that indicates no limitation of distance. The second of the two streams was at a later time persistently taken by him to be the San Francisco River, in western Mexico. If so, the journey from the Pima village thither could not possibly have been accomplished in the eight days that tradition allows for it.

Anyhow, after leaving the mountain lookout, the gold hunters traveled on for days — days that faded into one another with only endless mountains to wind through and unending passes and mesas to traverse, where the roadrunner sprawled in the coarse sand under bear-grass bushes, and where tall red bunch grass, mixed with the waving black-tipped stems of grama, half-hid curious antelopes. Then late one afternoon Gotch

Enough Gold to Load a Pack Horse

Ear led down to a stream lined with cottonwoods wherein millions of locusts were whirring that sound more penetrating to the ear than the race of rivet-drivers.

That night he directed: "Fill canteens. Before daylight in morning make horses drink. We leave early. No water tomorrow."

The morning was still fresh when they began climbing up beyond the altitude where the beaned mesquites and the prickly pears bearing black-red tunas were growing on the gulch floors. They saw their last covey of California scaled quail, and crossed a canyon cut through castellated red limestone. The guide said he had not seen the track of a man or of a horse for three days.

Then they came into a trail over which wagons had passed, some time before the last rain.

"Mark this road well," Gotch Ear halted to speak before crossing it. "It leads to the fort in the malpais rocks. When you need provisions, you can buy them in the store at the fort."

The fort has generally been taken to be Old Fort Wingate, the site of it being near the present town of Grants, New Mexico. But as to which direction it lay from where the Adams party crossed the road, no man knows.

[13]

Apache Gold and Yaqui Silver

It was away after dark when, on a canyon floor, Gotch Ear called a halt. He bade the men unsaddle, saying he would lead them afoot through a box entrance to a spring. They went through a narrow pass, watered, filled canteens and coffeepots, brought their horses back outside, and there spent the night. At dawn they saw their hobbled animals grazing in an abandoned Indian field skirted by a ruined irrigation ditch and growing a few pumpkin vines. This was the "Pumpkin Patch" that Adams and his fellow-searchers tried so hard in after years to locate.

The party now rode up the canyon in which they had watered the night before. In places, Adams said, it pinched in so that a rider could by stretching out his hands almost touch either side. Most of the way it was dry. After perhaps two hours' riding, they topped out on an uneven ground studded with lava rock and in places growing timber. On a high point Gotch Ear stopped and pointed to what frontiersmen called an "Indian post office" — a mound of rocks.

"Those sticks on those rocks," he said, "mean three Apaches went by here two days back. They will return."

All the men having come up to the "Indian post office," Gotch Ear now called their attention to "*aquellos dos piloncillos*" (those two sugar-cone shaped mountains) straight ahead, to the northeast. In the words of Adams, "they looked like two finely topped haystacks, daylight showing halfway down them."

"Those *piloncillos*," Gotch Ear went on, "are beyond the canyon of the gold. They mark it well always. Soon we shall go down."

Realization that the golden end of their trail was so near at hand brought a shout of joy from the men. The pace was quickened. Not long after midday the guide made for a long bluff, or palisaded wall. A man named Davidson who was riding in the lead asked the Mexican if they were going to climb that wall. He smiled and said, "You will see." Soon he passed behind a boulder that, from a short distance as well as from afar, seemed to be a part of the bluff. Behind this boulder, a *puerto*, or door — the famed "secret door" for which so many men have searched — opened through the rock wall. It marked the entrance to the canyon. The trail down, Adams said, was the roughest he ever rode. It made a perfect Z — a big Z, with variations along the bars of the letter.

Not until they had zigzagged a long time did they get a glimpse, which rocks and trees immediately cut off, of the canyon bottom. The sun was still more than an hour high when they halted beside clear running water, in a little level vale, just below some low falls.

Apache Gold and Yaqui Silver

"In the gravel by the water you will see the gold I have promised," Gotch Ear said.

Hardly had the men unsaddled before some of them were panning in the gravel. Immediately almost, wild yells of victory went echoing up and down the canyon. "Look at this" and "Look at that" were constant ejaculations while the panners held nuggets up to view. Several men who had no picks or pans were jabbing in the gravel with sticks, uncovering gold.

In the party was a German, commonly called a "Dutchman," who weaves in and out of nearly all stories of the Adams Diggings. "Poys!" he warned. "Do not make so tam much noises! Der Indians vill kilt us."

But the hilarious frontiersmen only laughed and yelled the louder. They considered themselves equal to any band of Apaches that might appear. No man among them had ever before seen such a quantity of free gold or ever before found water, wood, grass, game and gold all so conveniently arranged. This was paradise, the miners' dream come real. There was not much sleep in camp that night.

Gotch Ear was immediately paid his gun, ammunition, saddle equipment, two fifty-dollar gold pieces, two horses, the red silk bandana, with several knickknacks thrown in. He left in the darkness. What became of him is unknown, though there is a tradition that two

Tom Lea

of Chief Nana's Apaches were later seen riding the horses he took.

At any rate, the next day Nana and about thirty warriors appeared before the miners. They were not in a hostile mood, however. Nana told the white men that they might graze their horses and dig in the canyon below the falls, but that they must not go above, where his people were for a time camping. The canyon, he said, had but one entrance, the entrance the white men had come down, and was boxed — walled — at both ends. Whether what he said was true or not, the Indians seemed to have a secret way of entering and leaving.

Upon being questioned, Nana gave the name of the canyon, in his tongue, as Sno-ta-hay. Only a few of the Adams Diggings hunters have known it by that name, however, it being among them traditionally referred to as the Zigzag Canyon, the Z Canyon, Gold Canyon, Adams Diggings Canyon, and so forth. The stream sank in the gravel not far below the camp.

Several of the men did not have tools to mine with, but it was agreed that all gold found should be put into common accumulation, of which Adams had charge, to be later divided equally among the individuals of the party. The men who could not pan were put to cutting timber for a cabin.

Apache Gold and Yaqui Silver

There was one exception to the community plan — the German. His distrust of the Indians and of the situation seemed to grow every day. He asked that his part of the provisions be doled out separately and that he be allowed to work apart and keep his own findings. The other men were glad to be rid of his kill-joy company. He constructed a crude rocker and worked constantly.

About ten days after discovery of the gold, provisions began to run low. In a general consultation, it was decided that six men should go back to the road the guide had called attention to and follow it to Fort Wingate for supplies. Gold was weighed out for purchasing provisions, more ammunition, a whipsaw, additional axes, mining tools and various other articles. John Brewer was delegated leader of the detail. As it was preparing to leave, the German came to Adams and told him that he didn't like "the looks of things" and had decided to take his findings, go out with Brewer's guard, and stay out. He had between nine and ten thousand dollars in gold. His story will come in a little later. Brewer and his men calculated that they could make the round trip within eight days at the most.

The mining in the canyon went on, and the log cabin was far advanced in construction. In one end of it was a fireplace with an ample hearth. A part of the

[18]

hearth was made by a large but thin and comparatively light flagstone. It could be readily lifted out of place and reset. Underneath it, well sunk in the earthen floor, was a huge Indian mortar, made of lava, that had been found a little back from the falls — a vessel for pestling corn and dried meat in — perhaps hollowed out by prehistoric Indians. This mortar, or *olla*, was made the repository for the gold, and every evening such gatherings as the miners brought were put into it and the covering hearthstone replaced.

The weather was now falling, the nights growing longer and colder. The bluebirds, the return of which is the Indian sign of spring, were leaving the high mountains. The deer were at their fattest, and one hunter alone was able to keep the camp in meat. Indians came into view every day, but they showed themselves

[19]

so peaceably inclined that the customary vigilance against them was relaxed, though not abandoned. No matter whether prosperous or in desperate circumstances, some men grow restless, but with every panful of dirt paying and with the big Indian mortar under the hearth filling up daily, all the miners remained fairly constant.

Some of them had the notion, however, that above the falls the gold must be richer. The ledge — the mother lode with nodules of ore "as big as wild turkey eggs" — was located above the falls, and they wanted to work it. Yet Adams kept them in hand. He realized how serious a violation of the Apache instructions might be. One day a man who had gone after two strayed horses gave Adams an especially fine nugget to keep for himself. He said that in trailing the horses above the falls he picked it up. Adams reprimanded him and put the nugget under a chip at the base of a certain stump. Several stealthy pannings in the Indian territory followed. One man brought back a coffeepot half-full of gold.

The eighth day after the provisioning party had set out passed without their return. Adams was growing anxious. On the morning of the ninth day he detailed a guard to watch the cabin and took the man named Davidson to ride up the trail with him, determined to

travel until he found some sign of Brewer and his detachment. Right at the "secret door" they found the sign.

It consisted of five dead men, several dead horses, cast-away packsaddles, a whipsaw, flour scattered over the rocks, and other evidences of a surprise attack by Indians.

Without making a minute examination or finding the sixth dead man, Adams and Davidson hurriedly laid the bodies in a crevice of rocks and covered them with the packsaddles and rocks as a protection against wild animals until they could be properly buried. Then they turned to warn their comrades and prepare against an attack. That they themselves were not way-laid on the Zigzag Trail seems incredible. They re-called now that they had not seen an Indian for two days.

At a certain elbow, far down the Zigzag Trail, one could get a clear view of the cabin and of different spots in the gravel below. As Adams and Davidson neared this elbow, they heard wild yells — not from miners. Dismounting and keeping themselves hidden by boulders, trees and bushes, they swiftly crept to an outlook point. They saw, they estimated, three hun-dred Apaches, some on foot, some mounted, waving scalps and exulting over mutilated bodies. It was hardly possible that a single one of the men had escaped. The cabin was ablaze. Adams and Davidson figured that, in the Apache count of victims, they themselves would be missed and sought-for. They went back to their horses, threw their saddles into a crevice, and headed the animals down a side gulch where, they hoped, Apaches would in finding the horses be thrown off the men's trail. Placing themselves thus afoot seems now to have been a very foolish move, but horses are discoverable where a man is not, and Adams and Davidson felt sure that Apaches were above them as well as below them. In a thicket of quaking asps whence they could peep out into the valley, they now awaited darkness. While the hours wore away, they heard warriors evidently looking for them.

Before sundown they saw the Apaches withdraw from the vicinity of the cabin and go out of sight above the falls. In darkness the two escapes now undertook their whispered plan to steal down, at least get a drink of water, and secure what they could of the gold in the Indian mortar under the hearthstone. They moved with extreme caution and extreme fear. There must have been more than one hundred thousand dollars' worth of gold. Finally they reached the water and drank. Not a sound was to be heard, but their caution was not abated.

Apache Gold and Yaqui Silver

Crawling up to the cabin, they found that heavy rafters still smoldering had fallen right over the fireplace. The rocks were too hot to touch. Fifteen minutes of ax-work would have sufficed to remove the debris and a few buckets of water to cool the rocks. Yet one stroke of the ax and the sizzling from one bucket of water thrown on the hot stones might betray them. They were afraid to attempt the business. They found two canteens, one badly bent. After filling these and drinking again, they decided to remain a while in the hope that the fire would burn out enough to clear the hearth. But green pine smolders slowly. The hours of cowering and waiting seemed endless. Nevertheless, dawn was on its way. The "guide" to the morning star appeared above the cliffs. Love of life outweighed love of gold, and the fire still smoldered. At last they started back up the trail.

"Wait a minute," Adams whispered. He had suddenly remembered the nugget hidden at the base of a stump — the nugget that now seemed the price paid for the death of eighteen men and the ruination of a vast fortune.

He stole to the stump, only a few steps away, got the nugget and put it in his pocket. It, the gold carried out by the German, and whatever was taken by Brewer to buy supplies with, comprise all that the Adams Diggings are known to have delivered to the outside world. The story goes that Adams later sold his nugget in Tucson for ninety-two dollars.

He and Davidson knew of but one way to go — back over the route they had entered. They dared travel only at night. They had no food and were afraid to betray their presence by shooting for meat. They spent their first day of flight hiding on a rough timber-covered mound west of the "secret door." A part of the time they slept, taking turns in watching for Apaches. While on guard, Adams noticed again the *piloncillo*-shaped peaks and observed that to the left (north) of them a lower eminence had the shape of a bear's head. That night they got through the narrow canyon, found the spring of water, and emerged into the "Pumpkin Patch." During the day they gathered and ate a considerable quantity of acorns, but were afraid to build a fire to roast them.

From here on their progress became slower and slower, with many deviations. Still afraid to show themselves by day, at night clouds prevented them from seeing the stars to course by, while the rough country prevented their going directly anywhere. Some nights they probably made no progress at all. They were lucky in finding an abundance of piñon nuts, the very essence of food. Rains had left water in rock pits. Five or six

days after they left the Diggings, they struck the road that Gotch Ear had called upon them to "mark well." They did not strike it where they had crossed it, however, and they had no idea which end of it to take. But they knew they must follow it, and they did. One night they lost it but found it again.

Their feet were now very sore and Adams' shoes were so worn out that a foot bled from bruises. One day while Davidson was patching Adams' shoes with bear-grass fiber as they hid near the road, they saw through the bushes the legs of five Indians passing along. This made them more cautious. The afternoon of the next day, however, Adams said he was going to kill a bite of meat at any risk. To deaden the sound of his six-shooter, he took off his now ragged shirt and wrapped it around the barrel. He shot a cotton-tail rabbit. Not far away they could see a line of timber marking a stream. Before going down to it, they gathered some pieces of quaking asp, which in burning gives off almost no smoke, determined to make a fire by water and cook their meat.

It was still daylight as they roasted the morsel. Then they heard horses. They retreated into better cover, but soon discovered that the horsemen were United States troopers. The refugees revealed themselves, and were carried to Fort Apache, Arizona. They had been wandering for thirteen days, and were in a truly wretched and wrecked condition.

From here on, stretches of the story dim-out. Davidson was a much older man than Adams. There is an account of his having been at Fort Whipple not a great while after his rescue and having there told virtually the same story that Adams spread far and wide. In 1929 a woman in Flint, Michigan, who claimed to be a grandniece of Davidson, wrote that he died soon after escaping from the Diggings, leaving a diary and a map that located the gold in the Zuñi Indian reservation. Some men in Utah had an option on the map, however; their use of it by scouting over the Zuñi country in an airplane did not prove anything. So far as the Diggings are concerned, Davidson passed out of existence as soon as he left Adams.

While the two men were recovering at Fort Apache, sleeping in a tent belonging to one of the scouts, a noise startled Adams from sleep. His nerves were hair-triggered. Rushing out, he saw five Apaches, whom he thought he recognized as having been with Nana at the gold camp. His experiences had made him "jumpy." Acting on impulse, he grabbed his six-shooter and began firing. He had killed two Apaches before he was disarmed. These Indians, presumably the five whose legs Adams and Davidson saw from hiding, had come to the fort in peace. At this time there was no uprising among their tribe, and the United States troops were engaged principally in trying to keep peace rather than in warfare. Adams' rash act put him in the guardhouse to await military trial for murder. Two nights later he escaped, stole a black horse belonging to a lieutenant, and later showed up in Los Angeles. There a wife and three children awaited him.

Enough Gold to Load a Pack Horse

The fact that he was an outlawed man no doubt delayed his return to the Diggings, which had not yet taken his name and which he did not at the time regard as "lost." He knew, however, that to reach them and work them he must have a strong, well-equipped body of men. Gradually the Americans were conquering the Apaches, and every month of delay meant better chances for getting out the gold, although it was twenty years after the massacre in Sno-ta-hay Canyon before the last of the hostiles were penned-up and halter-broken. While he waited, Adams for a time ran a secondhand furniture store in Los Angeles and then a livery stable, but he seems never to have had any capital. He told other men of what he had seen and experienced, of the gold he had had his hands on. Such stories were by no means uncommon in California; yet listeners to them were never lacking. In telling his story to whoever would listen, Adams glided over geographic details. In the vast land of Apacheria, where Cochise, Mangas Coloradas, Victorio, Nana, Geronimo, and other chiefs led their swift-moving warriors, raiding, retreating, attacking, hiding, clear across Arizona and New Mexico and the trans-Pecos lands of Texas, and then far down into the Sierra Madre of Old Mexico, there were ten thousand canyons and double peaks. Adams was not giving away any golden secret.

[29]

II · "The Apaches Made Me Forget"

The first earnest listener that Adams found and decided to trust seems to have been a fellow member of the Masonic fraternity — C. A. Shaw, a Nova Scotian by birth, who had captained a Union ship during the Civil War and had after that cruised far and wide on a merchantman. His aim in life was to return to the Isle of Guam in his own ship, build a house with a deck all around it, and there retire. For him, gold meant Guam. Captain Shaw put up five hundred dollars, and a company of sixteen men set out. Adams tried to lead them over Gotch Ear's route from the Pima villages. In the end, he merely took a course that ended on the San Francisco River a hundred miles north of where Silver City was soon to boom as a mining center. This was in 1874, at which time the Apaches, desperate over losing their territory to the in-crowding Americans, were far more hostile than they had been ten years before. The expedition broke up before, as Adams said, "it had got good started."

The men with him were exasperated at his failure to remember landmarks. On subsequent hunts, as will be seen, similar exasperation almost cost Adams his life.

He would appear to remember, and then waver. His explanation to critics was boiled down into five words — words that became a saying over the Southwest:

"The Apaches made me forget."

Perhaps someday some point of rocks, some gap in the hills, a rabbit darting into a canyon crack, a piñon jay flying into a tree with a certain gnarled limb, would flash the familiar back into recognition.

He raised other expeditions. One spring about this time more than twenty men followed him out of San Bernardino, California, into northeastern Arizona, where for months they concentrated on trying to find the burned cabin. The search ended in violent dissension, several of the party accusing Adams of using them to get back into the gold country and then refusing to show what he recognized. Two or three years later a young man named Edward S. Doheny rode one evening into the camp of Charles M. Clark, near the present town of Payson, Arizona, looking for a job. He had come across from New Mexico, he said, and mentioned having noticed on his route, a part of it trailless, the burned ruins of a cabin in a canyon that, after getting down into, he found he could not cross. He had had to come out the way he had gone down. He knew nothing of the Adams story. Clark was full of it. He grubstaked Doheny to a horse-load of supplies to be used in going back to the cabin and digging under the hearth. But, as all the world knows, Doheny made his fortune in oil and not out of the Adams gold.

Some of the men that Adams interested in hunting with him went on searching the rest of their lives; others reviled him and became sceptics. Captain Shaw never wavered. No matter how mad, cracked, deceptive other men might say Adams was, Shaw knew he was honest and on one subject consistently sane and reliable — the gold. He checked Adams on many points. He traced down, for instance, the post trader who was at Fort Wingate in 1864. The trader remembered, he said, a party of six men coming in and paying in gold nuggets for supplies, then hurriedly leaving, saying they must hasten back to their partners "in the malpais country." Again, while Shaw was with Adams at Fort Apache one time, he overheard a veteran sergeant, pointing at Adams, say, "I could make trouble for that fellow." "How?" a soldier asked. "Years ago he stole our lieutenant's horse and got away." When told of this conversation, Adams replied, "We're saddling up and riding right now."

After Captain Shaw had spent all his savings, he got other men to back him. In tradition he is regarded as Adams' prophet. One of the men who backed him and prospected thousands of miles with him was Charlie Allen. Before he died in El Paso, in 1937, Allen wrote a pamphlet detailing some of the facts he had learned about the Lost Adams Diggings.

One time in the Seventies, Allen reports Shaw as narrating, Shaw and Adams were sitting in front of the trading post at Fort Apache when a band of Indians passed on their way to a night camp near at hand. They were being moved to the San Carlos Reservation. As they went by, Adams, deeply excited, pointed out Chief Nana. The two followed the Apaches to their camp and there managed to draw Nana into talk. He was, for an Apache, unusually talkative. He said among other things that he was not going to stay at San Carlos. Then Adams asked him how long it had been since he had been in Sno-ta-hay Canyon. Shaw said that Nana glared at Adams for at least a minute, boring into him with his eyes, and then without a word walked away, remaining absolutely unapproachable thereafter. It is a fact that Nana's Apaches were moved to San Carlos in 1874 and that some time later Nana, then over eighty years old, accomplished the most spectacular campaign ever made by an Apache chieftain.

Before being transferred to San Carlos, Nana used to spend a good deal of his time around the Warm Spring agency. The post trader there, a man named Chase, won Nana's confidence and liking. One evening while he and Nana were alone in the store, the outside door locked, he began counting his cash. He was entering the amount in his ledger when suddenly the Indian, who had been leaning on a pile of blankets, broke the silence by saying, "*Hermano* — Brother, someday I will take you to where there is lots of gold."

"Where is it, Nana?" Chase asked, looking up.

"In Sno-ta-hay," and the Indian gestured towards the northwest.

Chase turned over to the back of his ledger and wrote the syllables, Sno-ta-hay, down. Years later in Socorro, where he went to end his days, Chase showed the old ledger, with the name written in the back, to Shaw. He was never himself a hunter for the Lost Adams Diggings.

One of the strongest corroborations of Adams' story, considering the integrity of the man who gave it, was given by John F. Dowling at his home in El Paso, in 1927, not long before he died. He was a very quiet man, cautious, intelligent. He had been in the mining business — leading a life far removed from that of a wandering prospector — all his life. Not until he had grown blind and could only sit and wait did he tell what he knew.

In January, 1881, he was at Socorro, New Mexico, when a doctor named Spurgeon arrived there with a most demoralized crowd of Adams Diggings hunters. Spurgeon in looking for a man to trust was directed to Dowling, then young and vigorous and known among mining men for his capabilities. He gave Dowling this account.

"I was post surgeon at Fort Apache when Adams and Davidson arrived there after thirteen days of wandering. They were in a very serious condition both mentally and physically. I was called upon to care for them. I felt certain that Davidson would not live long. They told me, not very coherently, what they had been through. Adams showed me the solitary nugget

[35]

of gold he had brought out and gave a description of the country. I wanted right then to organize an expedition and go back with Adams to the gold. But the only people to organize were a few soldiers. Their orders did not include gold mining. I myself was under orders. Not long afterwards my term of service expired and I went to Toledo, Ohio, to practice my profession."

But Spurgeon could never forget the sight of the two human wrecks tottering into Fort Apache and the story they had told. As the years went on, he repeated the story many times to many people. The spell of it seemed to grow on him. Finally, late in 1880, he took leave of his practice and, in company with about forty other men he had persuaded to join him, set out for New Mexico. They had new rifles, new boots, collapsible water buckets, patented bedrolls, the finest equipment that Eastern supply houses could rig up. The train carried them to Las Vegas, then the railroad terminus. There they hired wagons to transport them to Socorro.

Spurgeon knew what life in the rough was; his companions did not. That winter proved to be very severe. Northers blew and blew. At some camps there was not enough water to wash faces in. The wagons bumped so over rocks that the newly booted adventurers preferred walking, and their feet became blistered and sore.

"The Apaches Made Me Forget"

The rough diet upset their internal systems. By the time they reached Socorro, in January, most of them were thoroughly disgusted, and the prospect of proceeding farther into an even rougher country, not at all inhabited except by Apaches, had no lure whatever. They sold their guns and gave away their collapsible buckets, and were for getting back to warm houses and bathtubs as soon as possible.

All except Doctor Spurgeon. He had entire faith in the gold. He was ready to go on after it, but he was so allied with some of his company that he felt compelled to return with them. After telling his story and explaining the situation to Dowling, he asked him if he would try to find the Diggings on a partnership basis. Dowling was interested, but when Spurgeon insisted on sending along one of his tenderfeet named Moore to represent Spurgeon's interests, Dowling objected. Dowling had made the acquaintance of this Moore and decided he "would not do." Still Spurgeon insisted, and finally the agreement was made. Spurgeon went back East. Dowling picked two hardy young frontiersmen who had worked under him and, with Moore, set out towards the West Fork of the Gila.

From the beginning there was friction. Moore upon arriving at camp would do nothing but throw himself upon his bedroll. One evening one of Dowling's men, named Al, said to Moore, "Say, stranger, if you're going to stop here tonight, yank up some wood." Moore did not budge. There were words. Dowling knocked up the end of Al's rifle just in time to make the bullet miss its mark. Dowling himself had come to the conclusion that Moore was not worth saving, but he did not want the trouble that a killing makes. Moreover, he had a genuine respect for Spurgeon and felt responsible to him for Moore's safety. The situation became more and more unpleasant, and a second time Dowling prevented a killing.

Two days after the first episode they came into a canyon that Dowling recognized as fitting the description of the Diggings. Moore saw nothing on the whole trip; Dowling's two helpers knew nothing. Dowling saw the stumps from which fifty or sixty trees had been cut — logs to make the cabin, he deduced. Then he saw some pieces of charcoal around a rough rock hearth from which the chimney had tumbled. Down the slope in the canyon was a waterfall.

"We'll camp here," he said.

It was still early in the afternoon.

Al came up close to Dowling. "Hob [the other helper] and I have decided we can't sleep another night in the same camp with that blank-blank Easterner," he announced. "We want to go back."

"The Apaches Made Me Forget"

"We'll all go back," Dowling returned.

He had located the Diggings. All he wished for now was to rid himself of the human incubus that made any positive work impossible. At this time, he later said, he knew nothing of the gold supposed to be hidden under the cabin hearth, or he would have contrived to spend the night in the canyon.

He headed his little band back, made a long ride to the next water, delivered Moore at Socorro and told him to go to Toledo and tell Spurgeon that he would hear from him later.

The conclusion is rather lame. "I needed money," Dowling related, sitting blind in his rocking chair forty-six years later. "We all tend to take the course that is immediately most convenient. I was offered a fine proposition down in Mexico. It was too good for me to turn down for a chance on the Adams Diggings. Besides, in those vigorous days, I was always wanting to get on the other side of the mountain. I went to Mexico.

"In 1907 I outfitted a man I trusted who knew the Gila country perfectly. I told him exactly how to get to the burned cabin. A few weeks later he returned, said he had found the ruins and made a thorough examination of the canyon for mineral. There was not a color of gold, he said. I concluded that, after all, I had not found the Diggings. Years and years went on. Then after I grew blind I accidentally learned that this trusted man had not gone anywhere but to a ranch run by some rowdies and had stayed drunk there until it was time to report back to me. I can't go anywhere myself any more, and now I don't believe I can tell anyone else how to go the way I once went."

Several summers Adams came to old Milligan's Plaza — now Reserve — on the San Francisco River, as a starting point for his questings. Three or four old-timers living there remember him. "The way his long, shaggy eyebrows hung down over his eyes made you think of an old Spanish mare with matted mane covering her face." He would never prospect alone, always got someone to grubstake him and go with him. One season, he hung for a time around Wash Jones's place. Barbed wire was just getting to be popular in New Mexico, and Wash Jones had fenced in about a section of land for a horse trap. Adams thought the Diggings might be in this pasture, and ventured out in it alone. But Will Jones, son of Wash, himself now both heavy and mellow with years, swears that "every time old Adams went out, he'd get lost, and before he could find his way back to the chuck table would have to follow the fence clear around that section of land." He was mighty fond of "mountain dew" too, but, drunk as well as sober, he always stuck to his story, without varying a single detail.

Along in the Eighties he brought a well-mounted and otherwise well-equipped company of Californians to Milligan's Plaza. They stocked up with provisions and were gone two months, returning very dry and disgruntled. After they had got a few swigs of whisky inside themselves, several of them began to make medicine in a bold way.

Cornering Adams, they came right out in the open with their plan. "You have not showed us one thing you promised," they said. "Now show or hang."

But two or three of the Californians protested that Adams had nothing to show, that he knew he hadn't all the time, and that there was no use in dillydallying about the hanging. They were actually about to string him up on a cottonwood limb when Wash Jones rescued him and put him in the mail hack bound for Magdalena. There he came under the protection of Bob Lewis, who had taken to looking for the Diggings long before this and was mighty glad to find the originator of them. Bob Lewis is night watchman at Magdalena now, grizzled and stiff but on occasion "as lively as a ga'nted two-year-old heifer."

The first night after arriving in Magdalena, as old Bob tells it, Adams got planted in a saloon and, with a fresh batch of listeners, launched out on his story. He wound up by swearing that if the commanding officer at Fort Apache had not refused him an escort, he could in 1864 have gone straight back to the Diggings and would now be "richer than Jay Gould."

Standing at the far end of the bar was a dilapidated, silent, but erect figure with hat pulled down. Bob Lewis said a man couldn't tell which suddenly flashed brightest — the scar on that man's face, running down from the outer corner of his left eye clear into his throat, or a knife that he jerked from his pants.

"You're a liar," the stranger yelled to Adams, at the same time pushing his hat back. "I was top-sergeant at Fort Apache in 1864. The post commander never refused an escort to any decent white man who had a reasonable claim on one. You are not only a liar but a horsethief. Gold! The only gold you ever had your claws on was off the bodies of men from California that you helped kill. By God, if I wasn't going to kill you, I'd prove you a waylaying murderer."

At this the scar and the knife both lunged, but Adams "joined the birds." The knife stopped before it reached the saloon door, but Adams flew across the street and down into the little railroad station, where he could barricade himself if necessary and from which

the train for Socorro was to leave in about an hour.
Bob Lewis followed him.

"I'll admit," Lewis reports Adams as having said,
after he realized the danger was all over, "that I lied
about Fort Apache. The truth is there is one thing
about the gold I have never told anybody and never
will tell anybody. But there is gold all right. Go and
look for the bones of those men who were carrying
supplies into the canyon. Show me the bones, and I'll
show you the gold."

Apache Gold and Yaqui Silver

For thirty years, "at odd times," Bob Lewis went on looking for bones. Then he found them — the skeletons of three men stowed in a rock crevice, pieces of packsaddles with them. This was in the Datil Mountains, not far from what Bob Lewis calls "Little Door Canyon." But he could find no gold. He had a partner named Pettibone who quit railroading to hunt the Adams Diggings "just one year" — and hunted them for twenty. Adams was long since dead, and his chief prophet Captain Shaw had at last grown too feeble to search longer and had retired into the Old Soldiers Home at Los Angeles.

There Pettibone went to consult him. He offered to buy him a ship to sail to the Island of Guam if he would direct the way to the gold from the bones. At the mention of his old dream Shaw brightened, but, "It isn't far," was all he could say. "It isn't far," he kept repeating. Soon after that, on August 15, 1917, Captain C. A. Shaw set out on that voyage of which no voyager has ever brought back log or waybill.

A final word about Adams. When Captain Shaw late in 1886 came to the home of Langford Johnston, who will further enter this chronicle, he said that Adams had that very year suffered a heart attack while hunting in the mountains of New Mexico, had been carried out to a railroad, and soon after reaching California died — on September 21. Captain Shaw, the Johnstons put it, "was too good a man to have faith in a scoundrel," and his faith in Adams was boundless.

A rancher of sixty years' experience in the mountains, where he met Adams and where he has observed many of his followers, deliberately asserts that Adams would have given up "the hallucination of his cracked brain" long before he died if people to whom he promised a share of the gold when found had not in return kept him "bountifully grubstaked with whisky."

The opposite of this view is expressed by a philanthropic soul named W. H. Byerts, whose knowledge of Adams, however, was only through the ubiquitous Shaw, with whom he also prospected. Byerts planned, if ever he found the Diggings, to stake out forty-nine claims — only one for himself, and one for each of the forty-eight state agricultural colleges in the Union. He believed in developing the soil. When he died in El Paso along in the Twenties, he left the Salvation Army all his property, including considerable real estate puzzlingly paid for in hard gold — and also a trunkful of his pamphlets, now become almost Biblical, entitled *The Adams Gold Diggings*.

"No man," Byerts wrote, "ever talked to Adams without feeling that he had a strong character and told only the truth. He would give the facts in such a positive and candid way that no one doubted his sincerity. He had seen a deposit of gold richer than that in the mines of King Solomon, the Klondike, or the fields of Africa. No wonder he spent the best years of his life trying to get back to such a storehouse. Over and over he warned mining men, however, that this gold was in malpais country, where ore is considered a geological impossibility. He doubted, therefore, if any regular prospector would ever find it."

It is time now to take up two other characters who were in the original Adams expedition.

III · The Man Who Was Not Dead

The leader of the six men who went from Sno-ta-hay Canyon for supplies was, it will be remembered, John Brewer. It will be further remembered that when Adams and Davidson found the bodies of their comrades, they counted only five, having no time to search for the sixth. They could not have found it anyway.

One time a mining man of Mexico told me that if ever I wished to hear the true story of a child-eating mountain lion, I should trail down an old-timer named Ammon Tenney. It took me five years to locate him, for he generally ranges in the most remote canyons of the Sierra Madre in Chihuahua and Sonora. All his life, not even counting out the time while Pancho Villa held him for ransom, he has been cowboy, trapper, hunter, prospector, a camp man of mountain and range. The panther, which Tenney shot just as it was about to spring upon another victim, has nothing to do with the Lost Adams Diggings, but it introduced me to a tale and a man that belong in the record.

While Tenney was yet a boy, his father sold out his cattle in Utah and moved down on the Little Colorado in the St. John's country of eastern Arizona and established the Windmill Ranch. One day in 1888 — only two years after Adams made his last hunt for the Diggings — an unusual caravan pulled up in front of the Tenney ranch. In the lead was a good wagon pulled by a good team driven by a man who had an eye that seemed to be searching every visible landmark. Behind him was another wagon in which rode his wife (a full-blooded Indian woman) and their daughter. A rope in the girl's hand led a horse, saddled and bridled. This horse she rode at times to help a horseman who followed with about twenty well trail-broken cows mingled with six Thoroughbred horses.

The owner in the front wagon said that his outfit had come from Colorado and that he would like to camp, rest up his stock, and "look around a little." Permission was readily granted. He said that he had been in that country twenty-four years back with some prospectors. He gave his name as Brewer — John Brewer.

In the weeks that followed young Ammon Tenney was with him much, and, as they scouted through the mountains, Brewer told him the complete story of his first expedition into that region, even turning over to him a manuscript narrative of his experiences.

Brewer's relation began with how a gotch-eared

The Man Who Was Not Dead

Mexican who had been captive to the Apaches led an expedition captained by Adams out of the Pima villages on the Gila River in 1864 to look for gold. The account, in short, corroborates the tale that has come down from Adams, though there are variations natural to diversity of witnesses and lapses of memory. Brewer's geography, like that of Adams, was confused and obscure. His experiences after the Apaches attacked his provisioning party were sufficient to explain any confusion; they will be given in Brewer's own words.

"I do not clearly know how I escaped. The Apache ambuscade was perfect. All at once dozens of Apaches were around us shooting and yelling. As I raised my gun from the sling where it was carried at the horn of the saddle, I was conscious of men falling dead behind me. Then an arrow that cut through the outer part of the calf of my left leg brought my horse down, and somehow in the fall I lost hold of the gun. I found myself in a crevice between big boulders headed into very broken ground where bushes and stubby trees helped to hide me. I kept going until I was played out. Then I crawled into a kind of place where a rabbit would be safe from either coyotes or eagles and waited until nearly sundown. No pursuers came near me. The ambuscade was early in the morning on the ninth day after we set out from the Diggings to get provisions. We had made a dry camp on the mesa the night before, as it would have been impossible in the darkness to ride and take pack animals down the Zigzag Trail.

"After I left my hiding place, it did not take me as long as I expected to get back to where the Indians had attacked us. There was still a little light in the sky, and I could see that the bodies of my companions had been moved. This gave me hope that Adams and the other men in camp were safe. I made good time going down the trail. The arrow wound in my leg was not serious, but now my thirst was raging. When I got to the point where I could look down on the cabin, I saw logs burning. Then my hope sank. Nevertheless I was ready to risk my life for a drink of water, and I went on down. I expected also to learn something from what was about the cabin. The gold stored under the hearthstone hardly entered my mind at this time.

"I slipped to the water and drank. Then I started towards the cabin. Suddenly I heard grass snap under what I took to be a footstep. I waited. Then in the dim light made by a smoldering log I thought I saw two slinking forms. I was sure they were Indians trying to waylay some escape from their massacre. I could not believe that any of the Adams party had escaped, and I felt positive that I alone of my party was alive. I crawled backward downhill, got again into the trail, and went up."

The forms that Brewer saw must have been those of Adams and Davidson. When Brewer gave his story to Ammon Tenney in 1888 he did not know that Adams had escaped and that his story of lost gold was famous all over New Mexico and Arizona. He had been for years trapping and ranching away up in Colorado, a quiet squaw-man far away from newspapers and talk. He had not been mining, and this was his first trip back in search of the gold. His narrative is resumed.

"When I got out of the canyon and again to the spot where the Indians attacked us, I almost lost my head. The terror and horror I had felt when I escaped all came back to me. I realized fully for the first time my solitary and desperate conditon. It was cold. I had not a match on my body, no gun, not a bite of food, not a drop of water. I was afoot and four days' travel by horse from any known civilized human being. I felt around for a while on the ground, hoping to pick up something of use that might have been dropped during the ambuscade. I got nothing but thorns in my fingers. I stood up with my knees knocking together and my heart pounding. I began running, I know not in what direction. I caught myself shrieking, 'Adams!

Adams! My God, what shall I do!' I had no idea of directions. In fact, I was just about insane.

"By now the night was far spent. Then I saw the thin moon coming up over a mountain. This at least oriented me, and I began walking toward the moon. The big mesa I was on allowed me to keep an eastward course, though I frequently stumbled into bushes. Once I ran and got a fall that knocked me senseless for a while and bloodied up my face considerably. When the sun rose, I was facing it. The knowledge that I was getting somewhere cheered me; the warmth was a wonderful blessing.

"I decided I had better hide myself in timber, but I could not sleep or stay still. After a few hours I began traveling again, taking advantage of whatever covert the ground afforded. Night found me utterly exhausted. I had entered a canyon in which I hoped to find water, but there was none. The cold kept me from sleeping more than a few minutes at a time. At daybreak I started up the canyon to hunt water. Within an hour I came to a pool. Near by were some berries that I tried to eat, but they were so bitter that my stomach refused them. The water, however, seemed to revive me. I kept traveling, losing much time keeping out of sight in timber or in gulches.

"When the sun was about three hours high, I came

into a wagon road. It is impossible to describe the relief
that the sight of wagon tracks gave me. They looked
to be at least a month old, but there were fresh horse
and burro tracks. Here was a route to civilized human
beings — to food and warmth and water. But following
the road, I soon saw moccasin tracks. This alarmed me.
I veered out, but tried to keep a direction paralleling
the road. About dark I lay down under some trees.
I was cold but slept a little. Then I awoke with sharp
pains shooting through my body. 'These are the kind
of pains that people die from,' I said to myself. I had
never felt anything like them before. It had been three
days since I had eaten anything except the bitter berries, but I had heard of men going for more than a
week without food. Cold sweat broke out over my
body. Again I slept fitfully and again felt the unspeak-
able pains. I was surprised when at daylight I could
walk fairly steadily.

"I knew that if I kept following the road to the east
I should eventually come to a Mexican settlement on
the Rio Grande. I resolved to get into the road and,
safe or unsafe, to keep it. About the middle of the
morning the road went down into a valley. A line of
cottonwood trees told me there was a stream through
the valley. As I rounded a curve, I saw a patch of
ground that had been planted in corn. Just before I

reached the little stream I saw two burros run across it. I lay down at the edge of the water to drink. No sooner had I swallowed than I felt deathly faint. When I opened my eyes, I saw three Indians standing over me.

"I did not care. I had no fear of them, or of death. The only feeling I had was gratitude at being somewhere where human beings lived. The Indians stood looking at me silently for several minutes. Then one of them spoke words that I could not understand. I made an effort to get up, but could get no farther than on my hands and knees. Then, to my great surprise, one of the Indians stepped forward and helped me to stand up, holding my arm to steady me after I stood.

"The only foreign tongue I knew was Spanish — and only a smattering of that. I thanked the Indian with the word *gracias*.

"He responded in the same tongue, saying, 'You are a little sick.'

"I knew then I was among friendly Indians. The leader proposed to take me to his house, pointing over a hill. I thanked him again. Another of the Indians jumped across the stream and soon returned leading one of the burros I had seen. But when that burro smelled me, he snorted and shied. The men tried to hold him still and help me on him, but soon gave up

[55]

the effort. Then, with a man on either side of me to steady my steps, we walked to the house.

"A squaw gave me some tea of a native weed, making me sip it very slowly. Then I was allowed some bites of meat and of beans. I wanted to eat more, but was prevented. The house was warm. Soon a great drowsiness overcame me. I lay down on two sheepskins and slept deep and sound — the first real sleep I had experienced in what seemed to me several lifetimes. I did not awake until the morning of the next day. Then I ate like a famished wolf.

"These people had no knives or forks. All their utensils were made of clay or wood. In the house, besides the three men, were two women and several children. I discovered another house near by and learned there was a village on beyond. News of my appearance and rescue had spread while I slept. Many people came to gaze on me. On the third day I was strong enough to walk with my host to the village, where, he said, the alcalde was waiting to see me.

"This head man spoke excellent Spanish. He asked me to tell fully of my experiences. This I did as best I could. The story of the great gold find did not interest the alcalde or any other listener nearly so much as my references to the Apaches. They would not think of making up a party to return to the gold canyon, or to venture into Apache territory. They spoke of a fort somewhere to the west, but I could not understand where or how far away. I do not know what tribe of Indians these were, but they were one of the Pueblos. When I said I wanted to get to the Rio Grande, they replied that by going on east I would strike that river and the big road leading to Santa Fe. They insisted that I remain with them until my strength was fully recovered.

"I stayed about a week. Then my chief rescuer and host guided me several miles east and left me in a trail that would, he assured me, lead to the Rio Grande. It did. Just before dark I looked down on the cottonwoods lining the river. All day as I walked alone, I kept thinking of Adams and of my other companions. I have never fully justified my leaving the canyon without being more certain of their fate. However, had I delayed a day longer, I never could have made it to the friendly Indians.

"At the place where my trail struck the Rio Grande lived several Mexican families. One of them gave me bountiful hospitality. The next day I followed a trail up the western bank of the Rio Grande for several hours before I found a crossing. On the east side was a village. I remained here three days and then received permission from the *caporal* of a pack train to accompany his outfit to Santa Fe. Our rate of progress was that of a worm. We never made more than ten or twelve miles a day. When we came to good grass and water, we recruited the beasts, all of which were poor, for a three or four day stretch. It took us a month to get to Santa Fe. I got a job with a freight outfit going to Missouri. It was several years before I returned West, and then I kind of took up with the Utes in Colorado."

Such was the story that John Brewer not only told but sketched in writing for Ammon Tenney a half-century ago. He felt sure that Gotch Ear had guided the Adams expedition across the Little Colorado River. Three years before Brewer arrived, Captain Shaw was at the Tenney ranch while prospecting in eastern Arizona. Brewer could no more locate the way to the Adams Diggings than could Adams himself or than the faithful Shaw.

In 1928 Colonel C. C. Smith, U. S. Army, retired, who had marched and scouted all over New Mexico, in commenting on the Brewer-Tenney narrative gave it as his opinion that Brewer struck the Rio Grande at Las Lunas or Belen. Wherever he struck it, he was a long way and a crooked way from the gold.

"The Apaches made him forget" also — the Apaches and a quarter of a century.

IV · The German

There are as many stories about what became of the German as there are canyons in which the Adams gold "ought" to be. He is generally referred to as "the Dutchman," and through him the Adams Diggings is often called the Lost Dutchman Mine, though there is another great lode by that name. The most summary and simplest disposal of the German's case comes from Bob Lewis.

On one of his many prospecting trips into the Datil Mountains, Lewis fell in with an old Navajo chief named Secretare — a kind of renegade to his tribe. Riding along, they came upon the disintegrated skeleton of a man. It had evidently been weathering for many years. "That is the damned German," old Secretare grunted — and said nothing else. He seemed to know.

But tradition no more than history will rest as simply as bones. That the German took out a heavy quantity of gold when he left the Diggings with the provisioning party all reports agree. Charles Allen in his evidence-sifting pamphlet avers that he had exactly sixty-three pounds and three ounces of gold, which he sold to a storekeeper named Hinton at Yuma, then bought cattle with his money, took up a ranch near Prescott, and was there killed by Apaches in 1867 — too soon, in that era, to go broke and need another stake. Most of the stories agree that the German took up ranching; but maybe the Apaches did not kill him and maybe he was sure of his purpose when he declared he was leaving the country for good.

The German was solitary, not at home with the rough frontiersmen, bent on avoiding trouble with the Apaches. With his stake made, what more natural than for him to return home, go back to Germany? And this he did — as Clem Smith found out.

Clem Smith left Idaho in 1933 to find the Diggings. He knew rocks, especially the processes of crushing them. He had a map traded to him by a Mexican who claimed to have secured it thirty years back from Byerts — Byerts, whose pamphlet on the Adams gold has been memorized by hundreds of seekers. Well, it did not take Smith very long after he "got on the ground" to become convinced that the Mexican had lied about the location. He quit trying to follow the map and followed his nose.

Then, away up in the Mogollons, he and his burros nosed into Old Alphabet Young and his burros. He is known over a wide stretch of country as Doc Young, and for a decade or more he has been "ninety-two years old." He goes about the country with two burros carry-

ing a stock of Indian herbs that, taken "with faith," will
cure any ailment known to man and make the partaker
live to be as old as an eagle. He is psychic and many
times has "seen" Adams digging at his Diggings; so he
knows exactly how the gold canyon looks and will be
able to recognize it when, "this coming summer," he
finds it. He has "gathered more facts about the Adams
Diggings and the German than any man living." He
knew Captain Shaw well, found him once at a spring
stone-blind in a sand storm, cared for him and restored
his sight with some of the herb tea.

Clem Smith and Doc Young told each other what
they knew, and decided to throw in together. A season
was enough for Smith; he could not stand the "psy-
chism." But he will always believe that Young's story
of the German is true. This is the story: —

About 1898, Young made a considerable stake of
money and went to Los Angeles to see the sights. One
sunshiny day while he was sitting on a bench in a park,
an old man came and sat down beside him. Soon the
two were talking, and the talk easily drifted to mining.
The Lost Adams Diggings was inevitable. The old man
then told of his long interest in that great lode, and said
that he had located the escaped German in Heidelberg,
Germany, but had been unable to get a satisfactory
response from him by letter. Young was at the time

about to set out in search of the Adams Diggings. He had the money to go to Germany. He went. He found the German, Emil Schaeffer by name, and was convinced beyond all doubt that he had been with Adams.

The German described the canyon of gold as being boxed at both ends, a great sunken trough, overlooked by two haystack peaks. He expected the Apaches to attack, for they had warned the Adams party not to get reinforcements and not to think of settling. When some of the men left while others went ahead putting up a cabin, that meant to the Apaches more whites to come and seizure of the valley. The German said that he took out approximately ten thousand dollars in gold, but that some of it was from California. He was on his way from California to New York when he fell in with the Adams crowd. Now that he was free from them and the Apaches, he kept going and did not stop until a ship landed him in Hamburg. In Germany ten thousand dollars was a fortune. He prospered, married, raised a family.

"Not for all the gold in that uncivilized country," he said to Young, "would I go back to America. What good would more gold do me, anyhow?"

No offer would budge him, but he gave the best directions he could after being for thirty-five years away from an unknown and then uncharted country,

and Young came back to take up the quest he will not abandon until he dies. The directions the German gave him could not possibly be very clear. Taking them from old Doc Young and using his own theories, Clem Smith has decided that the Diggings are in the Apache Box, twenty-two miles northeast of Duncan, Arizona — a long jump from the post office — a wide place in the road — called Adams Diggings, on the Quemado plains of New Mexico. Anyhow, the Apache Box is fairly convenient to Lordsburg, where Clem Smith gave me his evidence.

Let the Dutchman rest in peace.

V · The Man Who Knows

Fourteen years ago I was put on my own kind of trail to the Lost Adams Diggings by a story published in an El Paso newspaper. It was a reprint of the Byerts pamphlet. Everything inside me that goes out to adventure was moved. That part of me will not die, I think; but what interests me most now about the Adams Diggings is the men who have sought it. I have sought them in many places.

In 1937 a newspaperman in Albuquerque advised me to step up the street and see a druggist with an Italian name. He looked as if he might have smiled once when he was a baby. "Be here tomorrow at ten o'clock," he said.

I reported at the hour named. The old druggist ordered a Mexican boy to conduct me to the house of "el Señor Gray." We cut through an alley. In five minutes we were going up a flight of stairs, in the business part of the city. The Mexican boy looked through an open door into a long living room, wherein I saw a thin woman with gray hair and a drawn face sitting in a wheel chair.

"El Señor Gray?" the youth asked.

The woman pointed to a door at the right end of the

room. The Mexican urged me towards it and at the same time ran back the way we had come. I went through the door into what is correctly called a "den."

As I entered, the stubbiest man not fat that I have ever seen was coming out of an adjacent bedroom pulling on his breeches. He was in a short-sleeved undershirt and wore house-slippers over white socks. His enormous head was rolling under a lion's mane absolutely white. Even impeded by his not yet adjusted breeches, he moved with the alacrity of a Spanish bull. His eyes, as dry as gleaming steel in their brightness, spoke to me before he uttered a syllable. I forgot to speak. After he had, quickly but without haste, surveyed the intruder from head to foot, he ejected a few words as if he were locking the door of a steel vault.

"What do you want?" was all he said.

"To hear you talk," was all I said.

"If your time is not too valuable to wait a little, I will talk."

"It is not too valuable."

By now he had his breeches buttoned. He tossed his mane and sprang through the door. I heard him say, "Come on." His tone hadn't changed. Presently I heard the sound of table implements clicking against china, but not a word. I surmised that the dining room was at the other end of the living room and that the two were eating breakfast, though for an active man ten o'clock has always seemed to me as late for that meal as it is early for the next. I sensed that a Mexican woman was waiting on the table.

The den in which I waited seemed at first glance to have nothing in it but pictures, hundreds of pictures, hung and pasted from floor to ceiling, the walls abso-lutely covered — pictures of horses, horsemen, scouts, Indians, a cowboy (whose "face and shirt," Gray later commented, "were when the photograph was taken clean at the same time for the only time in his life"); pictures of mountains, volcanoes, canyons; most of all, pictures of girls, scores and scores of female heads and female figures in every garb from Eve's to Mohamme-dan swathing. Also the room was littered with Indian baskets, guns, pistols, maps, swords, daggers, books, pot flowers, and smoking materials. There were two comfortable chairs and a desk.

When, after having been gone not more than twelve minutes, James B. Gray — I had learned his full name from a label on a catalogue of photographers' supplies — entered, I stood up. He gave me a swift glance, and I could see that he was more comfortable with himself.

"Talk about what?" he asked.

"The Adams Diggings."

We both sat down. It was after two o'clock before I got up to leave the room. When a man talks for four hours like a blocky dun horse plunging through black chaparral chasing an outlaw steer, a listener can learn a lot about him. At the end of that time I knew a lot about James B. Gray, but I was no more sure of what is deep inside him than from looking at his features and watching his movements I could have guessed his age. What I tell about him is what he told me. I have never talked about Gray with a soul who knew him, or consulted any records.

In the Eighties he was chief of scouts on the Apache Reservation of the Chiricahua Indians in Arizona. He learned about Indians from them. In 1892 while he was working for the Three H outfit in southern Arizona, owned by Senator Hearst and associates, a Yaqui chief named Kelzell from across the Sonora line brought him a buckskin sack of gold nuggets and said, "We trust you. Buy guns and ammunition for us with this." Gray went to Denver, sold the gold, took the money to New York, and bought two hundred and fifty U. S. Army rifles, new but of a supplanted model, at three dollars and forty-five cents each and a million rounds of ammunition at one cent each. The stuff, marked "Agricultural Implements," was shipped by boat to Galveston and thence to Tucson, whence it was taken out, two or three guns and a lug of cartridges at a time, until it was all across the border in Yaqui hands. After that, with Gray laying the ambuscade, the Yaquis trapped a whole regiment of Mexican soldiers and annihilated them.

Kelzell the Yaqui said, "When you have a need, call me and I will pay with my life if necessary." Gray did not ask Kelzell to show him where the nuggets came from. He has always been a great lover of horses. While on the Three H, he had a very fine mare that he prized as a Bedouin prizes the mare out of a line possessed by his family for three centuries. One day he missed this mare. He trailed, read sign, learned something from a *vaquero*. The thief was the Apache Kid. For three days Gray followed the tracks. Then he found the mare dead. The Apache Kid had ridden her until she could go no longer. Then he had killed her and cut one of her loins out for a steak.

Gray went to the Yaqui Kelzell. "I want the head of the Apache Kid," he said.

Without a flicker, the Yaqui answered, "That is hard. It will take time."

In the darkness three months later he appeared before Gray. "It is in this sack," he said.

It was.

Gray was with the Rough Riders, and one of the pictures is a sketch, made by Gray himself, of Teddy Roosevelt. In time he came to be a photographer by trade, though he has retired from that business now. He fought with the Japs at Peking and his chief interest in life now is seeing them overpower China. He traversed Algeria and Arabia, and has a complete file of the *National Geographic*. He found the ruins of Yucatan before excavations were started. With a pack mule he used to roam for months at a time, alone, exploring the Indian ruins of the Southwest. He has read all there is to read on the Island of Mu and the Lost Atlantis, and he wanted to expound to me his theories on how the civilized races of America came from Egypt. He was in Belgium when the World War broke out and there made a wonderful demonstration of marksmanship against the Germans; later when the United States Army

would not take him because of his age, he won a medal for service with the French. Years ago he wrote a book on the War designed to be published only after the death of General Pershing. He is something of a linguist.

While he was in the border country, he hunted the Montezuma Mine, the Padre Mine of Sonora, and the Pegleg Smith Mine, which is undoubtedly somewhere between Yuma and Warner's Ranch. All he ever actually found were the bleached skeletons of a man and a horse beside a cap-and-ball pistol and two hundred and nine dollars' worth of gold. He does not claim to know where these great lodes are. He does know where the Lost Adams Diggings are.

Other men may put up fronts of assurance, but Gray is the one man I have met who has no doubts as to the location of the Adams gold; the one man also who has brought some of the gold out — and has no idea of going back. Because he is an intense Rosicrucian, and cares nothing for more money, is not the only reason he will not go back for that gold. I have delayed his story because it cannot be separated from the man. Here it is: —

"Adams had two accounts. They have been confused with each other and mutilated by bad memories and ignorant credulity. One account he gave when he was vigorous and fresh on the trail — before he got into New Mexico; the other, when he was decayed and cranky. Sometimes, too, no doubt, he told the story in a way to throw others off his track. The true Adams story is this. Part of it I learned from the Apaches.

"At the Mission of San Xavier near Tucson, in 1864, Adams and ten other men met the young half-breed Indian who said he could lead them to gold. The 'breed's mother was a Spanish woman who had been captured by the Apaches; his father was God knows who and probably his mother did not. He had been with the Chiricahua Apaches under As-ces-ta-ce-la, who was a little younger than Mangas Coloradas and Cochise. I don't know how Adams and his outfit came to find him or what sort of trade they made with him. Anyhow he agreed to lead them to the gold.

"They left Tucson headed in a general northeast direction — eleven men, besides the guide, with twenty burros. They travelled slow — from eight to twenty miles a day — for eleven days. They crossed two good-sized streams, probably the San Pedro and the Gila, and got deep into mountains — the mountains in what is now the Apache Reservation, in Arizona. This I am sure of.

"On the afternoon of the eleventh day the half-breed led them into a deep canyon. After they had followed it some distance, they turned up the left fork. About sundown they camped at a place where the walls were sloping back so that mountains could be seen towards the west. Adams said he noticed the striking resemblance between one mountain and the form of a woman lying down on her back — her breasts, throat, head, all distinct.

"The next morning the half-breed said, 'Here's your gold.'

"The men ran to the dry wash gravel and began panning. They found sand and nuggets in extraordinary quantities. For two days all hands worked fiercely. All knew they had a bonanza. They must prepare to hold it and work it out. It was decided that nine of the men should go back to Tucson for supplies and tools, and that while they were gone the two other men, Adams and his partner Davidson, should make a rough stockade cabin. The nine men left. Adams and Davidson went to building the cabin. It was a half-dugout — a good windbreak with a sheltering roof. It had a fireplace.

"Under one of the rocks of the hearthstone was a cavity about thirty inches long, twenty inches wide and eighteen inches deep. That-sized cavity will hold a lot of gold. It was meant for the gold in the gulch. Before the twenty-two days it would take the nine men to go to and return from Tucson had passed, Adams and

Davidson had not only made the cabin with the fireplace but had put a lot of gold in the cavity. They had not seen an Indian.

"About sundown on the twenty-second day, they heard yelling and shooting in the direction from which their companions would return. They knew what that meant. Each grabbed some gold, a gun, and a canteen, and bolted. They found that all the nine men had been killed. Then came a wandering that lasted for days. They were lost, half-starved, all but perishing of thirst. Finally they appeared at old Fort West on the Gila River, which was near the present town of Cliff, New Mexico.

"Adams went to Tucson and cashed the gold he had brought out — about half of what he had gathered, he said — for twenty-two thousand dollars. He spent that and the rest of his life trying to refind the mine. I don't know anything about the German they put into the story.

"A man who says, even today, that he is not afraid of the Apaches and certain other wild Indians is either a fool or foolishly ignorant. When I was chief of scouts on the Apache Reservation, I could command the natives under me, but I was always conscious of being watched. As I scouted, I was always looking for gold, just keeping my eyes open and saying nothing.

The Man Who Knows

"One day while riding in a canyon, I knew I had at last come upon the Adams Diggings. I saw the ruins of a cabin; beyond I saw the beautiful breasts of the mountain woman, throat and chin. I was conscious of special scrutiny on the part of three scouts riding out a little from me. I hung my off-foot under the fore-leg of the pony I was riding so as to make him appear to step lame. Then I got down, lifted his foot as if to get out a rock lodged in the frog, picked up a stone to knock with, and otherwise fooled around until I gathered four *chispas*, — "sparks," — as the Mexicans call little nuggets. I was very casual and did not linger. I thought I had not been detected. A curious circumstance ended this day's business. About the time we got into camp, my horse went to limping on the off fore-foot. I found a sharp-edged rock worked into his frog. It was a piece of quartz so heavy with gold that it was better than a nugget.

"The second time I went to the place I slipped off alone — I thought. I had secured three good nuggets when I was jumped. I don't know how many Apaches were in the crowd. They were a good way off. I picked off a pony or two, nothing else, taking care not to hit a man, and left. I afterwards sold the three nuggets for sixty-two dollars.

"When I went back the third time, I was out of the

service, though still hanging around the country. I should have taken my stag-hounds along as warners, but I did not. My horse was usually as good as a dog to sense Indians. But this time he did not scent the Chiricahuas until they were upon me. You don't know how soft an Indian can move — as soft as a little green snake gliding along a leafy twig after a gnat. One of those Chiricahuas could steal up on a man as easily as the shadow of a buzzard passes over prairie grass. I had a whole handful of nuggets when I looked up into the muzzles of a dozen rifles. I had picked the nuggets up swiftly too, for I did not intend to stay long.

"They already had me tied to a sapling and the dry wood was piled up about me, when old Go-sho-nay, a White Mountain medicine man with whom I had been *muy amigo*, saved my life. He came out of nowhere, it seemed to me. I had to promise never to try to come back so long as the land remained Apache territory. It still remains Apache territory. I have kept my word. Leaving honor aside, I think it wise to always keep it.

"If you ever meet a white man who has lived in that neck of the mountains much, you'll find he don't talk. Old C. E. Cooley married two of the Chiricahua squaws. He never did talk.

"Maybe you have cut the trail of Captain R. C. Patterson?"

The Man Who Knows

I nodded and did not interrupt to tell of the many times I had cut his trail.

"While I was still chief of scouts, I met Patterson one day. He knew where he was going all right. I told him to turn back. No, he was going on. 'Do you know how close you are to a six-foot hole?' I asked. 'Maybe not.' 'Then look.' He looked into the rifle barrels of six scouts who wore nothing but a bandelier and a gee-string and whose horses were hidden. Patterson turned tail and never came back. Those Apaches followed him and casual-like showed themselves, one at a time, in front of him until he crossed the reservation line. It was my duty to turn Patterson back; if it had not been for me, his dust would be in the reservation yet. I thought that in taking the lead in putting out a prospector I would gain the confidence of the Apaches. You have heard how well they trusted me.

"Yes, I could go back to the canyon now all right, but I'm not going and I have no desire to go."

When I passed through the long living room on my way out, the thin gray woman was still sitting there in her wheel chair — just sitting. On the street I saw a sign proving that my body was in Albuquerque, New Mexico.

VI · Where the Gleam Led
Captain Cooney

Years before the Apaches could be cleared out of
their New Mexican stronghold, Jim Cooney entered it
and made a gold strike in the canyon named for him.
Then in 1880 a band of Victorio's warriors got him.
His brother Michael Cooney came out from Louisiana
to take over the properties.

He was an Irishman, which means that he had imagination and optimism, and also a congeniality for politics.
People called him "Captain." The first thing he did was
to blast out a tomb in a great boulder forty feet high,
place the body of his slain brother therein, and then
seal it up with a marble slab inscribed in a marble style.
A hundred years from now that mausoleum will no
doubt still be the show place of the country. Next,
Captain Cooney drafted a dispatch to the young and
gay Silver City *Enterprise* announcing that Mogollon,
over the mountains from Cooney Canyon, held "the
wealth of the world." He had an interest in the strike
there. Then, with Morris Coates as a partner, he began
looking for something even richer than the "wealth of
the world" — the lost Adams Diggings. He was a kind
of spiritualist, and he used to wake Coates up of a morn-

[78]

ing to tell him where a vision in the night had revealed the gold.

Before long he was hunting by himself. Then he quit the search to go up to Santa Fe as a legislator. There a story he heard put him back on the trail that was to lead him deeper and deeper into solitude and finally through the door that never opens outward.

The story he heard goes back to the early Eighties, when the western boundary of Socorro County, bigger yet than some states, was being surveyed. Along with the surveyors was a boy whom two or three of the ax-men took to deviling unmercifully. He was sensitive, and one day after these tormentors had goaded him to desperation, he left them swearing he would never go back to camp. Unarmed, with nothing but the clothes on his back and a pocket knife, he took out across the mountains in the direction of Silver City, towards the southwest.

On the very first day of his foolhardy flight he came to a canyon of running water. He was very thirsty, and it happened that the spot where he got down to the water was immediately below a waterfall. While he was kneeling to drink, he could see the base of the bluff over which the water plunged, the cascade making a kind of curtain that hung out a foot or more in front of it. Back in this sheltered recess a ledge of "color" caught his eye. He broke some pieces off and put them in his pocket. By a miracle he got through to Silver City. There he showed his samples to a mining man named Burbank, keeping quiet to everybody else. Burbank had the samples assayed. They ran one hundred and fifty thousand dollars to the ton. Nuggets as big as *frijoles* were imbedded in the rocks.

The boy wanted to go back at once, but Burbank would not risk the Apaches. He did risk them in another direction, however, by going with Langford Johnston in another direction. After the Indians had killed Burbank, Johnston buried him and came back to look for the "Lost Boy Mine." Burbank had not told, or had not been able to tell, him much about the location, however.

Meantime the boy had gone to his home in Saint Louis. There he stayed two years before returning to develop his find. He found Burbank dead. The memory of men who had abused him and cut his soul to the quick came back. He would not have another "pardner." He was used to being alone anyhow. He had a little money. He outfitted and set forth alone. It is known that he made camp between Sycamore and Turkey Creeks in the Mogollons. He came back to Silver City once, posted a letter, got supplies, and slipped out again.

Where the Gleam Led Captain Cooney

The letter was to an uncle in Kansas City, a printer. In part it read: "I have found the richest mine in the world. The country is so rough I cannot get my pack outfit nearer than three miles to it, but I have blazed a trail from my camp to the ledge. The Apaches are getting thinned out, but I write you in case . . ."

Maybe the Apaches were getting thinned out, but the thinner they became the more desperate and relentless they grew. The boy never came back.

It was the printer uncle, with the boy's letter, that Captain Cooney met in Santa Fe in 1892 while he was attending the legislature. Captain Cooney certainly must have known that the boy's ledge of gold was not the placer gold, picked out of gravel, that Adams had found. Nevertheless he somehow identified the one with the other. He felt sure that the Boy's Canyon — as it came to be called — and Adams' Zigzag Canyon were identical. Henceforth there was to be no surcease for him in the quest.

The boy had not been seen for ten years when Captain Cooney located three trees blazed deep on the divide between Turkey and Sycamore Creeks and found indications of a camp. That was all. He could find no trail blazed anywhere, and there was not a waterfall within many, many miles.

Then, the ledge of gold under a canyon waterfall –

and the Adams Diggings in the same canyon — must be somewhere else.

Captain Cooney had no "pardner" now to awaken in the morning with news of a directing vision. As the years went on, he became more and more a man of utter solitude. Perhaps his closest confidant was a chunky little pack burro named Black Pete, with whom he habitually shared his beans and sourdough bread. Many a morning he would say, "Which way, Black Pete?" And whichever way the little burro pointed his ears would determine the direction of the day's search.

There were quiet nooks like Dutchman's Spring, away up close to the Continental Divide, where Black Pete seemed to like the wild rye particularly well, and many a time Mike Cooney would spend a day traveling to such a place just to humor his burro. Then on a summer morning while he was waiting for the sun to come over the peak and warm his joints and dry the dew off his bedding, he would sit around and watch the hummingbirds suck the wild horsemint or fight a pigmy battle. What sense was there in hurrying anyhow? Besides, the whole country was good to prospect in, for everybody agreed that the Adams gold was not in a mineralized area. While Black Pete got slicker and fatter, the aging Cooney must have spent uncountable hours dawdling around camp doing nothing but watch

a striped chipmunk peel seed out of a pine cone. He would whistle at a squirrel to make it bark, and then the two would keep at each other until the squirrel quit. Crossing some valley, he liked to stop and watch the wild turkeys grazing on the beans of the tall pink-flowered turkey weeds, which hard-pressed squatters nowadays cut and haul into their chicken yards.

At night he had for solace the flickering patterns made by the light of his campfire on the great tree trunks and the boulders and drifts of straw on the ground. Again he would look out in the moonlight upon the mountains beyond — always mountains and always beyond — standing gray and mystical, as ungraspable as the stars, their roseate peaks shading down to a blue rose lost in inky black shadows.

Some years were dry, with the thunder of August a mockery and only the flirt of a canyon wren to reveal a tin cup of seep-spring water — too dry for the wild dewberries and raspberries. Then prospecting was a cramped business, but generally it rained on the mountain crags when it didn't rain anywhere else. Pink Mexican primroses bloomed waist-high alongside goldenrod more golden than gold and mixed with Indian pinks as tall as the wild cannas and the great asters. Out of rain clouds there was a great wind, and at night there was a great moon.

Apache Gold and Yaqui Silver

The whole world was buoyant, and the lode of gold had to be great, and certainly it was within reach — somewhere. Clouds that hung like flags down in crags a day's climb away seemed to signal "It is here." Zigzags of chain lightning forking into a bluff beyond an abysmal canyon seemed to semaphore "It is here." More than once after a storm he saw that strange and rare phenomenon, a double rainbow — and it was a doubled sign of hope.

In this gigantic world overlooking gigantic chaos, under gigantic moons and winds, growing gigantic flowers and trees, any man who belonged — who had become a part of the land — could have only gigantic dreams. And the longer Captain Cooney lived in such a world, lived in solitude with his own quest and his own visions for company, the richer and more real to him became the Adams Diggings.

He would never hunt in the lava beds, but he circled all around them. He hunted in the red bluffs of the Zuñi country, where the boys who herd goats stand like sentinels hour after hour on the cliffy points and, looking out over the forbidding waste lands, seem to guard some secret — a secret more mystical than material — that only their eyes have seen. He stood on Inscription Rock, where the name of Oñate carved with a dagger-point still attests that he passed here in 1606 — Inscription Rock, which a canyon splits open and out of which the winds, the sands, the rains, the ices, the snows and the suns of unnumbered thousands of years have carved castellated pillars more Sphinx-like than the pyramids of Egypt. He stood there and looked towards Mount Taylor to the east and the Zuñi Buttes to the west and wondered which way Adams passed. He climbed the astounding butte called Acoma, where the Indians have their "city in the sky," the loneliest and eeriest point of habitation north of the Andes in the Western hemisphere. Somewhere, in all the immense world of mountains and canyons spread out beyond, the Adams gold lay waiting. He could wait too.

One summer he decided to prospect into the Taylor Mountains, away to the north of his usual haunts. He always liked to get up high so that he could see out. From his camp he watched the golden mist of sunset fade slow, slow on the Sandia Mountains fronting the Rio Grande a hundred miles east. The mystery, the vastness, something forever undefinable in such vistas, lured him back to the Mogollons and the Tularosas. There he could gaze upon familiar crags out in the pure blue — blue above them, blue around them, blue under them, clear down to where jags of white scarred the blueness.

William Henry Wright, the great observer of grizzly

bears and recorder of their ways, came to the conclusion that in the Selkirks they bed and loiter on the heights partly at least to enjoy the grand views, which they spend so much time seemingly contemplating. It must not have been altogether fear of enemies that caused Indians of the Southwest to build their homes on the most inaccessible mountain tops, far from wood, water and tillable soil, but also a desire to look out. Captain Cooney, of Irish blood and of Louisiana swamp experience, came to belong to the mountains as truly as grizzly bear or Pueblo Indian belonged; and many and many a time he worked up to the summits for a look beyond anything that a miner could ever touch with his pick.

Gold is where you find it. Though the old prospector may not so realize, the trail he follows is in many places covered up by the Romany pattern. And so, for Captain Cooney, it was on and on. Prospecting down some prong of the Gila River, he would get as low as the mistletoed cedars, and then begin working back up again — into junipers, the alligator bark around some of them hiding tree-rings dating back to the time when the sequoias of California were saplings and the footprints of Christ were fresh on the sands of Galilee — from junipers into oaks and pines — out of oaks into great Douglas firs mixed with gigantic pines, the air

about them ever as fresh as the mountain ferns growing in the shadows, and beyond the level where piñon
jays warn the deer of a man's approach. Then around
patches of quaking aspen, dazzling in the sunlight, into
a waste of black, volcano-smelted rocks, acres and
acres wide, not one sprig of vegetation visible amid their
sterility.

On some eastern slope of these summits Captain
Cooney would stand or sit and gaze for hours at the
vast spread-out Plains of San Augustine, the flecks of
blue shadows and the intensifying sunshine on the
grass making it look as white as a freshly laundered
sheet. The Plains of San Augustine seem destined to
preserve the character of Magdalena as a cow town,
but nobody ever dug gold out of them. Still, as Captain Cooney used to tell, when he saw them glistening
and luring far away, he could never keep from thinking
that his friend Beauchamp might be right.

Beauchamp was a kind of "jack-jeweler," in Clifton,
Arizona. He claimed to be a seven-months' child, and,
therefore, to have powers of divination. He had maps
and more maps. He would buy any waybill a Mexican
tried to sell him. Every summer he would go to Mogollon, outfit, and, maps wrapped in oilcloth, strike for
the canyons running down out of the mountains into
the San Augustine Plains. To him every crag and

canyon draining into the Plains of San Augustine was a
possibility for the Adams gold.

Captain Cooney had far rather watch an eagle soar
and mark where its shadow skimmed the ground —
ground hiding gold — than be where men might watch
him. Sometimes when he was going down for provisions,
he would turn aside from the trail and "lay low" until
a rider he had sighted was past. However, there were
not many riders to meet. He did not like the inquisitive-
ness and curiosity of most people. No man likes to have
the deepest thing in his nature, the purpose of his life,

made light of. More than that, the years of solitary living were making him shy, like a Tarahumare Indian who will slide behind a tree to keep from being detected, or like a deer that instead of running in fright will merely cover himself with a bush and watch. He would go out of his way, though, to meet lone hunters like old Ben Lilly and Nat Straw and Ed English, so as to ask them if they had noticed the leaning pine with Adams' initial cut on it, or about some other feature of the mountains.

But when the ice binds the high-up world and snow covers it depth over depth, the elk, deer, birds and other creatures have already come down — all except the bear, and he is sleeping the winter through. Man must come down too. As a rule, Captain Cooney wintered on his old stamping grounds along the San Francisco River. Cooney Canyon, of the famous mausoleum, empties into it. Adams had time and again come to the San Francisco, looking for his own trail — and that made the valley a better place for Captain Cooney to linger in.

When he could look out and see on the mountainside a brown patch that had been white, he began to overhaul his equipment and watch for the sure sign of spring's opening. That sign, good for both season and luck, was a wild turkey-hen setting. Whenever he could spy or hear of a nest, he was ready to head out. This was as a rule along towards the first of April. Meanwhile, waiting for the long winter months to pass, he usually heard something to increase his fervor. Maybe it was nothing but another talk with Charlie McCarty, up at Milligan's Plaza, who had kept one Adams party from getting lost, helped them run out of whisky, and in the end traded for the very horse that Adams rode. Captain Cooney was on the San Francisco when Bear Moore's body was found.

The facts that came out about Bear Moore gave him immense encouragement. During Bear Moore's lifetime everybody who knew him was certain of just one thing — that he wasn't knowable. He always wore long whiskers, which, like his hair, were matted with bear-grease and dirt. He might have his hair roached once a year, but never his whiskers. He kept them to hide two sets of scars on his face — one set from a knife, and the other from the claws of a grizzly that gave him his Christian name. He lived out in the mountains no-body knew where, occasionally showing up at Pinos Altos or Silver City with gold, which sometimes he sold but usually shipped to the mint at Denver. One time in Pinos Altos he got twelve hundred dollars for a buckskin bag of flour gold — gold fine in grain like flour. He did not come into the settlements of a winter;

people said he holed-up like a bear, living on meat he had killed and put away. He was never known to possess a horse, mule or burro.

Then Nat Straw and another prospector found Bear Moore's body not far from his camp. Under his chest, clutched tight in his hands, was a baking-powder can half full of black sand mixed with flour gold and also containing a big nugget. The camp proved to be a cave, the ash heap at it six feet deep. People figured he had lived there for twelve years. It was two miles from any water, as remote and unapproachable as the walled-up cavern of some prehistoric cliff-dweller. It was estimated that Bear Moore must have buried at least one hundred thousand dollars of minted gold. Whatever he buried is still where he put it.

His cave held a kind of clue to the source of his gold — a set of rawhide horseshoes. He himself never had any use for any kind of horseshoe. He had long been accused of being a friend and ammunition-supplier to the Apache Kid. Therefore, those rawhide horseshoes must have belonged to the Apache Kid, who often used such. The Apache Kid must have brought gold to Bear Moore.

I know four men, out in New Mexico today, each of whom claims to have been in on the killing of the Apache Kid at four widely separated places. I wonder how many men in Arizona shot him. His best biographer says he was not shot at all but died a natural death. He ranged all the way from the White Mountain Apache Reservation in Arizona down into the Sierra Madres of the Sonora Yaquis, and east to the Rio Grande. He was more of a killer of Apaches than of whites, though for years whenever a lone prospector or rancher in Arizona or New Mexico was found murdered, the Apache Kid got the blame. At times other renegade bucks were with him, but generally he was alone except for some young squaw he had kidnapped. Customarily, he kept the squaw only a short time, sometimes — after his wild, fierce, ever-attacking and ever-dodging way of life had worn her out — leaving her free to work her way back to her people; again he killed her, so that she would never talk; always, as long as he kept her, he tied her to himself at night with a rope so as not to risk betrayal.

When he was not in a region too rough for any horse to travel, he rode the best horses the country afforded. When a horse could no longer carry him, he killed it and cut out the loin-straps to eat. Before he became this pariah of the tribes and races of two nations, this Ishmael of mankind, womankind and beast, the Apache Kid had been foremost among the native scouts at San Carlos in Arizona, had learned the white man's language, his way of preparing food, and his expert marksmanship. At the same time no warrior of Geronimo's band, no lone wolf among the remnant of Chiricahuas yet hiding like wild dogs in the mountains of western Chihuahua, ever attained to more cunning in tracking an enemy or covering up his own tracks.

Not even a gold hunter who waylaid ghosts would dream of trying to take the trail of the Apache Kid. Nevertheless, to Captain Cooney the gold that the Apache Kid presumably brought in to Bear Moore and the gold that Bear Moore most certainly possessed went further to prove that gold lay somewhere — somewhere where Adams wandered — waiting to be found. Captain Cooney had additional evidence.

One of Butch Cassidy's "Wild Bunch," who had drifted down from Jackson's Hole in Wyoming to work on the W S range along the San Francisco, told Captain Cooney of an old Indian trail leading around Bullard's Peak. The description made Cooney think it might lead to Adams' Zigzag Canyon.

The trail had been traced out, though in many places the tracing was only a shadow, generations back by Apaches who wanted to travel unseen. It dived into impassable cracks; it went over a hundred feet of steep-sloping, solid, slick rock where more than one horse had started sliding and shot to his death far below; it hugged cliffs and twisted through fringes of timber. Finally it went down into a tunnel-like canyon, a thousand feet deep from rim to bottom, so narrow for an hour's travel that a rider threading it could in many places reach out his hands and touch the walls on both sides and at the same time look up and see driftwood lodged far, far above — a sight to set any man speculating on the result of a cloudburst at the head of the canyon. But this trail took the old quester only to a rincon where a horsethief in no way related to the Apache Kid had some horses shod with rawhide.

In the summer of 1914 Captain Cooney decided that if he went to Socorro and worked back westward, instead of as usual starting in on the San Francisco to prospect eastward, his luck might change. It did. In October somebody ran across him away up in the blue. Next May, three searchers located his skeleton. In his vest pocket was a brief diary, the last entry in it: "*Nov. 15* — Let in a little sun." Also there were four or five little nuggets evaluated later at twenty-six dollars. They could hardly have come from the Lost Adams Diggings.

VII · Hounded Hunters

The men who have been lured by the Adams Diggings are of two kinds: the regulars, signed up for life,
and the volunteers for some special campaign.

The regulars, mountain rats, confirmed prospectors,
will for years by the tens, unremittingly, with unflag-
ging expectations, thirst, starve, freeze on the endless
trail and over trailless ways beyond which the mirage
beckons. Yet deep in their natures they are not so
much after the gold as they are inexorably bound to
a course of life. "If I were worth millions," an old burro
tracker of the Black Range, who has read books and
looked within himself, wrote me, "I'd still be here in
this camp, tramping the hills, looking for gold, always."
The prototype of the kind was Old Kentuck, who,
after hunting the Diggings for years and years, finally
sailed away with a pardner from Patagonia for Punta
Arenas with the idea of outfitting a ship there and steer-
ing on into the Antarctic seas to find an island with a
volcano spouting nuggets of gold. Half of these regulars believe in ghosts; nine out of ten in signs, and all
in luck — a luck pronounced impossible by geology.
Most of them, being natural men, are queer, eccentric,
cranky.

Hounded Hunters

A letter from one of the volunteers with a perspective, Fred Winn of the Forestry Service, at Tucson, will reveal the two classes in juxtaposition. "The century was still young," his letter reads, "when I went out with an old Scotch sourdough by the name of Hackberry Campbell and two burros to hunt the Adams Diggings, mostly in the San Mateo, Datil and Magdalena Mountains. I was not dedicated to live forever on the trail — and a mighty cold trail it was — but I have known numerous otherwise level-headed forest rangers, cowmen, barkeeps and sheepherders — yes, level-headed sheepherders — to become locoed with the Adams Diggings and leave their firesides, campfires, cattle, coin counters, sheep and families to take up the search.

"Hackberry could quote the Good Book like Leviticus himself and could outcuss any bullwhacker that ever freighted over the Santa Fe Trail. He insisted on a full supply of Bear Canyon Dew, carried in jugs with corncob stoppers. As he was boss and as I had agreed to furnish the grubstake, we were liberally supplied. A little of that brand would go a long way and a high way. Once we ran entirely out of grub and several times we all but froze to death, but the Bear Canyon Dew never entirely evaporated. Hackberry had a map on buckskin which, one time while he was about

[97]

seven-eighths seas over, I copied. I don't know what he ever did with the original unless he finally traded it off for booze. We went down into every canyon and dug into every old prospect hole in an area of half a million acres, more or less; but as Hackberry always kept the map carefully guarded and as I was afraid to reveal my copy of it, it could not be identified with a single landmark. It could have been put to better use as a poncho to keep out the cold. Before I quit, I learned that every shack and adobe house in the Southwest was where Adams stopped on his 'last trip.'

"We threw in for a while with Horned Toad Ab Johnson and Sixshooter Charlie. According to common report, Johnson often got so short of chuck in the course of his prospecting that he ate horned toads. Hence his sobriquet. Several years after my grand tour of the Adams Diggings country, I ran into Sixshooter Charlie on the Arizona line. He was cocksure he could lead me to the gold up in the Navajo Reservation; he had positive evidence that Adams' supply party had come in from that direction to the place now called Gallup. All these fellows are gone now. I hope they have met Adams on the Happy Golden Shore and there staked out a claim at least half as rich as the one they expected to find here."

Colonel John B. Crawford was not a regular either. He owned silver mines and stock and silver mines all over the West. He was a plunger and a gambler; one night in Denver he gambled away $75,000 in stacked coin. His brother Joe Crawford was chief engineer for the Pennsylvania Railroad. He himself was known clear to Boston. When, during the panic of 1893, silver was demonetized, Colonel Crawford went broke. The only way he could recoup his fortunes lost in silver was to turn to gold. He had salvaged enough money to hire two clerkly scouts. He set them and himself to gathering and sorting out all the data available about the Lost Adams Diggings. At that time there was probably even more "information" floating around on the subject than there is now. The gatherings were assembled into manuscript form, totaling, it is claimed, about seventy thousand words. When the evidence was all in, Colonel Crawford decided that the Diggings must be in southwestern Utah. He raised an expedition and prospected for five months on the trail he had mapped out. Then he burned the manuscript.

Another irregular was another colonel — Colonel Jack Fleming of Silver City, who at one time owned the finest saloon in the "city," was mayor, and had his mining interests rated at half a million dollars. At a livery

how he managed to stay on, five scalps that he had taken in one killing hung on a rawhide string in his cabin. He was "as peculiar as they make 'em." His ranch was a night stand for the buckboard mail that came to operate between Magdalena and Reserve — the line over which Adams was once whisked away from a gang of his own men determined to hang him.

"One night," relates Montague Stevens, rancher, "I was on the buckboard that stopped at Patterson's ranch. My sole fellow passenger was a drummer, and after supper Patterson unloaded many of his Western experiences on this stranger, who was very much impressed. The next night we put up at the same hotel in Magdalena. Two days later we were sitting on the plank sidewalk in front of the hotel when Patterson, who had driven in his wagon for a load of supplies, came walking along. The drummer jumped up, shook his hand vigorously, and asked after his health. Then he continued, 'And how is Mrs. Patterson?' 'That,' Patterson curtly replied, 'is none of your damned business,' and he walked on. The drummer was still further impressed."

At a lake he made by damming up a spring flow, Patterson planted an orchard that became a landmark. He was thrifty and enterprising enough to have always both a home and a good outfit for prospecting when

spring opened, and from the day Adams stopped by, showed him a piece of ore, and gave him his story, he lived to hunt the Diggings. At first he prospected at random. Then he blocked out the whole Navajo and Apache countries with the idea of covering them section by section. He never could make sure in his own mind which tribe destroyed the Adams miners. (How the Chiricahua scouts with James B. Gray turned him back from the Apache reservation in Arizona has already been narrated.)

Apache Gold and Yaqui Silver

In 1888, he advertised that he was raising an expedition, free to all entries, to invade the Navajo Reservation and take possession of the gold. Between thirty and forty men joined it. It was a topic for headlines in the New Mexico newspapers. Montague Stevens was at the time rounding up steers on his Horse Springs range to fill a contract. His boss and three other cowboys quit to join the gold-getters. After a good deal of dissension, the expedition got to a Navajo field from which they took "one squash that was a full load for a mule." A country that could grow squash like that must produce at least hen-egg-sized nuggets. "Captain" Patterson pointed jubilantly beyond some mountains. They went on until they had run slap out of whisky, had no provisions left, not even squash, and were in a dry canyon. Then two reservation officials rode up with notice either to get out or to prepare for battle with U. S. soldiers. They got out. Patterson left, satisfied that the gold was farther on in the direction he was blocked from going, but since he couldn't hunt there, it might be somewhere else — and until he died he kept hunting it somewhere.

Langford Johnston was "running" twelve hundred head of cattle on the San Francisco River in western New Mexico when one day in 1886 the never-resting

Shaw appeared unto him. "You have been recommended to me," he said to Johnston, "as an honest man, an Indian in the woods, a good shot, and an expert trailer. I need a pardner. I will tell you the story of the Adams Diggings." He told it. Johnston gave Shaw a home and hunted with him until Shaw, thirty years later, was too feeble to go out any longer. Shaw swore that Adams confided to him something he had never told another soul. He in turn imparted this secret to Johnston, who kept it until he died, in 1931 — still yearning for "one more trip."

Johnston once made a good stake out of a copper mine at Clifton, but he was interested in only one mineral, gold, and in only one form of that gold — the Adams gold. He usually took from one to seven men with him. One time, while Powder River Jones was along, a chunk of rock fell from a cliff and rolled in front of him. Powder River's eye caught a glint. He picked the rock up and showed it to Johnston. "Gold all right," the leader ejaculated, "but it ain't Adams Diggings ore. Ride on." Another time he found a good vein of horn silver in the Mogollons. He rode on. Years later, hard up for money, he decided to return to the silver for a grubstake. He found that another man had been making good money out of the vein for five years.

Apache Gold and Yaqui Silver

While he was searching, Mrs. Johnston would stay at home and raise her children on cornbread and game meat. As the boys grew up, they joined their dad. In old age Mrs. Johnston would night after night get out her ouija board and ask it, "When is Langford going to find the Adams Diggings gold?" Invariably the reply would come back, "He's almost at it now." Her fidelity to the gold was as steady as her fidelity to her wandering husband. "The Adams Diggings is our religion," she would explain.

When Langford Johnston was in his eighty-third year, a mining man who has for half a lifetime been gathering all that he could hear or read on the Adams Diggings and transferring it to typewritten sheets with all the proper names codified so that nobody else will learn the secret — sent the old seeker a map. In the reply that came back were these words: "Last night I got to looking at your map and building air castles, and all the old love of hunting for the Adams Diggings came back on me. I could not sleep at all." No other seeker probably has ever had the geography of the route to the Adams Diggings, and indeed the whole story, so well-detailed as had Langford Johnston. He began the search when he was forty-one years old; he and his wife had nine children; he hunted with avid faith for forty-three years.

Hounded Hunters

Walk-along Smith was an enigma to everybody who knew him, and nearly everybody over an enormous territory west of the Rio Grande knew him either directly or by report. He would stop at a ranch where he liked the air and stay for months, earning his keep by teaching the children reading and writing and 'rithmetic. Once in a while he would winter in Socorro or Reserve or some other town, giving music lessons for a modest fee. He never killed a rattlesnake, just watched one, as he watched all other creatures of nature. He was never known to have his hands on a gun. Generally he did not tarry long anywhere, just walked along. He carried neither baggage nor canteen, though it was known that he carried script. When he came to a habitation, he would talk freely of where he had been, but he would never even intimate where he was going. An hour would come, perhaps in the night, perhaps in the day, when the people would realize that he was gone. A year or three years later he was likely to reappear and then again disappear. People wondered how he could pass over some long stretches of country without dying of thirst. Several times in his later years he was found by automobiles and horsemen in a perishing condition.

So far as anybody knows, Walk-along Smith never prospected, but it was no secret that he was gathering complete data on the Adams Diggings. In particular he was making a circumstantial list of all the men who had died or been killed in search of it. He wrote down many facts. He had ears to hear not only the words of human dwellers but also what the chipmunks under the pines, the bluebirds in the junipers and the antelope under the rim of the lava beds had to tell. He was well read. He was seen more than once in the archives in the ancient Governor's Palace at Santa Fe, where to the attendants he was an unnamed mystery.

He had often said that when he died he wanted nobody to know it and that he hoped his body would never be found. I was in Magdalena late in 1937 when word came that Walk-along Smith's dead body had been found out from Lordsburg, between the road and a mountain that he had apparently been making towards — probably to die concealed, as he had often planned, in a cave. Then something of the enigma of this queer character's life was solved — for some people. Walk-along Smith was Billy the Kid! The Kid, men who had held the secret close-locked now revealed, was not killed by Sheriff Pat Garrett. What was buried in the coffin at old Fort Sumner was two bags of sand. Sheriff Pat Garrett and Governor Lew Wallace, realizing the character back of Billy the Kid's outlawry, sent him off to a far-away school! Years later he returned to New Mexico, a quiet, penitent, charitable man, who would not kill even a rattlesnake and was bent on living only the life contemplative. And eventually he was going to deliver the Adams Diggings over to the cause of charity. Billy the Kid's ghost has walked in many forms.

One victim of the Adams gold that Walk-along Smith had down in his list was a Harvard graduate named Walter Walter. Tuberculosis had driven Walter from the east to a log cabin in the Medley range. The climate remade him. The vast country took possession of him. Then the Adams Diggings claimed him. Periodically he would go back East to visit his people, but the visits were always short. He was affable, but mostly he lived alone in his cabin, and alone he hunted the gold. The range lands knew him as The Hermit.

On several occasions he sold small amounts of dust and nuggets. One day he showed nuggets to Bowlegs Payne, who has chased cows under the mountains most of his life. "Throw in with me, Bowlegs," he urged. "I've come now to where I can't play hermit and accomplish what I'm after. I've been on the edge. Look at that gold. The next trip I am going into the greatest lode in the history of the world."

But Bowlegs Payne was not interested. He had heard that story before. The Hermit set out alone on a chunky dun horse with a black stripe down his back — "the race that never dies." He led a pack pony with the same kind of bottom. He did not come back. It was known that his hunting ground was towards Acoma. He had probably been dead for months before anyone missed him. A brother in the East, who had often jested at the idea of something as outstanding as the Adams Diggings being lost in any kind of an explored country, came down. He hired men who knew the mountains to help him find his brother. After a search that extended over months, he learned how that vast country can swallow up a man as well as a mine. Years later a skeleton identified in some way as Walter's was found, near it the bones of a horse. The theory — and it was nothing but a theory — was that The Hermit had got too close to the Diggings for the satisfaction of ever-guarding Indians.

There will never be any way of telling how many men who have gone in to find the great Unfindable have not come out. The number is no doubt much smaller than popular conception has made it. I have heard of a few not-returners whose cases it would be redundant to record. The death of mystery — and therefore of drama — has been mostly to the solitary. The Apaches did not confine themselves to prospectors. The only human beings they spared were lunatics, whom superstition made them leave alone. Unlike some other people, they did not put searchers for the Lost Adams Diggings in this category.

VIII · The Malpais and Some Maybes

From New Mexico's Rio Grande east far into Texas and from the same crooked line westward across Arizona, malpais — lava — rock appears intermittently. The 'way-back, authorized native pronunciation is *mal-y-pie*. Often the rocks lie sparsely scattered on good soil, float from some flow of prehistoric ages. In other localities the rock is continuous, making the true "badlands." The most noted of these badlands is an apex-shaped "slaunch-and-dicular" area angling from the Santa Fe railroad, skirting it at Grants, New Mexico, — near which was located old Fort Wingate, a mere spot now called San Rafael, — to a point some fifty miles southwestward; in no place is it more than thirty miles wide. Coves of boulder-strewn earth and outjutting headlands of fire-blackened lava make the outline of the area as irregular as the fjorded and promontoried coast of Norway. This is *the* malpais.

Towards the north of it there are numerous extinct volcanoes, from which the seas of fire once flowed. Geologically there were two flows, the second, lying to the east, too recent for the elements to have disintegrated it. In it are pits of glazed walls so steep that only a creature of four padded feet would attempt descent to their barren floors. Horrific chasms, made by the lava's contracting when it cooled, cut and crisscross the beds so that a person trying to progress in a certain direction will be twisted into labyrinthian isolation. Such places are impassable even for burros. Growing in seams of dirt that it has taken untold centuries to lodge between adamantine blocks, grama grass waves its rich black seed not a hundred yards from the bones of a cow starved to death on the drouth-stricken plain just beyond the malpais' edge. That lava will cut a pair of rawhide shoe soles to shreds in a day's walking.

The malpais of the old flow is a more negotiable region, but for any unguided stranger, no matter how experienced, an awful land. Forests of pine reach out into it, broken by canyons and dikes of lava as barren and forbidding as they were a million years ago. In these canyons are the famous ice caves, glacial frigidity and infernal fire combining and with the reserve of almighty power saying in symbols of silence: THOU SHALT NOT PASS. The ice caves afford the only water known to the region, except in time of rain and snow. Deer and rattlesnakes that inhabit the land seemingly do not require water. Mountain sheep, once common, have been killed out.

The Malpais and Some Maybes

My first approach to the malpais was from the south, where a few wells out from the lava's rim afford water, and the sheep of a Basque owner graze over an area composing a quarter-million acres. His shepherds, some of whom see a town hardly once in five years, move camp with their only home packed on a burro, their lives as lonely as that of the lone Ancient Mariner on a lone ship on the wide, wide sea. At a kind of sheep camp commissary I found in charge a half-breed Cherokee Indian who wanted to know something about mineral laws. According to him, two nesters from back in the hills somewhere had found "a showing of gold" in the malpais, though they could not get to their location with any beast of burden.

At Paxson Springs, a log-loading siding on the northwest side of the malpais, I stopped to inquire about the lay of the land. The only man visible seemed anxious to talk. He saw an Indian mortar in my car; at once he was all interest. He must show me some Indian things he had found in the malpais. His name was Frank Childress. If I would go on down to Agua Frio, hardly a half-mile distant and in a malpais nook, I'd find good water to camp by and another hunter for the Adams Diggings, named Chalk Lewis. Thus it came about that I went into the malpais next morning, horseback, with two men who have spent the prime days of

[113]

recent years searching for gold hidden by lava.

In the worst part of the badlands we came into a kind of trail, a crooked line, rough lava underfoot but the larger boulders rolled aside, that must have been made before any English-speaking man set foot in New Mexico territory. Stumps of pines a foot and a half through and living pines even larger obstruct the trail, the roots having somehow found lodgement, though in places of unbroken lava nothing leafy can live. Then we came to the ice cave at which these men had made a location — a cavern apparently formed by lava roofing over a canyon. Not many steps down into darkness, and one is treading on ice, against great boulders of ice. Moisture sweating out of the roof has formed billions of crystals, suggesting egret feathers, fern leaves, snowflakes and all other fairy forms of whiteness and delicate tracery that one can conceive. Not a square yard of the floor is level, and the icy inclines are slicker than glass.

Here, they say, was one of Geronimo's holdouts. Next to the ice at the entrance are wagonloads of charcoal. Did the Indians bring down wood to melt the ice? There is no water, no dripping of water. The ice never melts unless artificial heat is applied. Back in the cavern has been found pottery pronounced by scientific experts as belonging to extinct tribes of Indians,

perhaps the people who about 1000 A.D. built the astounding structures in Chaco Canyon. Out from the
cavern are a few crude corrals of lava rock — Apache
shelters. Reports of explorations notwithstanding, no
one seems to have gone very far into the roofed canyon
of ice. The Adams Diggings hunters I was with had
dug down in the cavern and "discovered some kind
of mineral" decidedly not gold. A small ice cave near
the edge of the malpais can be approached by car; it
is much less interesting than the one I saw, beyond
which are others.

Such are the caves and such is the malpais concerning which prospectors for the lost gold have brought
back reports as marvelous as the one old Jim Bridger
used to make about the Petrified Forest — "putrified
trees standing up with putrified birds in 'em, a-singing
putrified songs." About the only people who go into
certain parts of the malpais are prospectors, and absolutely the only kind of prospectors who go are looking for the Lost Adams Diggings. They have been responsible for a widely believed description of ancient
cliff-dwellings hanging on the walls of a watered valley
glimpsed accidentally by two or three white men, always unable to return to it. They have told of another
lost valley in which a Scotchman used to live distilling
whisky that he traded to Indians for nuggets secured

near by, though the Indians would not allow him to take the gold out. They have told of a nest of desperate outlaws allied with a few never yet subjugated Apaches and Navajos who from a secret oasis in the malpais guard the only entrance and kill any stranger who tries to enter. Since the Adams gold can't be found where men can go, it must exist where men can't go.

Yet reports of small amounts of gold brought out of the malpais by Indians in recent times are many and persistent. My friendly guides, Frank Childress and Chalk Lewis, knew a man named Moore who, about 1890, traded a logger out of three teams of horses and a nugget valued at sixty dollars which Moore's widow still has. Moore would not take the horses unless the nugget was thrown in. The logger told how a Navajo with whom he was very friendly kept saying there was gold in the malpais, though he would not show it. Finally, the Indian agreed to get a piece of gold to prove his assertion. He took the logger to a certain place in the malpais and told him to remain there, not to follow. The logger stayed as directed. He had a watch. In exactly thirty-six minutes the Indian returned with the sixty-dollar nugget. A second time the Indian took the logger to the same spot, gave him the same directions about not trying to follow, and twenty-eight minutes later returned with another nugget, smaller than the first.

Persistent rumors of gold in the area caused the United States Government early in the Nineties to have the country geologized. The geologists reported that there was no gold and that there could be none unless under the deep overlay of lava. Prospectors do not dig at random through hundreds of feet of granitic hardness looking for a mineralized rock that will invite them to dig deeper. But geological opinion has merely tended to strengthen in some seekers the belief that the Diggings must be in the malpais. Did not Adams say over and over that his gold was not in a mineralized formation and that no geologist would ever find it? Gold is — always — where you find it. Adams also said that the gold was in a malpais country — and lava rock detached from the malpais beds is scattered from Dan to Beersheba.

"It ain't a question of finding the Lost Adams Diggings," Horned Toad Johnston used to say with bishoplike assurance; "it's a question of recognizing 'em when you see 'em."

In the malpais or out of the malpais, why can't the gold be found? There is in the Southwest no such thing as a canyon that a man with a pick and a burro has not picked into or walked over. Indeed, there is hardly a canyon in New Mexico or eastern Arizona that some version of the Lost Adams Diggings has not led directly to. Has nature covered up the gold?

Sixty-five miles northwest of Roswell, New Mexico, are the prehistoric ruins called — erroneously — Gran Quivira. Judging by the remains of aqueducts and reservoirs, archeologists believe that at one time several thousand people lived here, though now there is no water within a long distance. A tremendous upheaval of the earth from which a flow of lava spread seventy miles southward apparently destroyed not only the water supply but habitations and people. No such change in the surface of the earth within modern times has occurred to cover up the Adams Diggings.

But a landslide could have covered it up.

"Give me my burro, my pipe and a few good books," Jason Baxter, with the saltness of time in his voice and face, used to say, "and I'll never be lonesome, no matter how long I am on the trail."

The Nigger Diggings, the Snively Diggings, the Schaeffer Diggings, the Adams Diggings are "all the one and the same," he used to hold, "and the Baxter Diggings too, if you want to call them that, only I never dug."

He and John Adair were striking in the direction of

where they figured the Diggings lay, away up north of the Datils, when the water they had counted on finding in a canyon failed them. That night a Mexican mule broke away; the next morning its trail showed leading towards a lone mountain off to the northeast. Along in the afternoon they caught up with the mule, piled a load on it from the other two mules, now weakening, and turned the seemingly waterwise creature loose to go its way. Away off to the northwest could be seen the White Mountains of Arizona. The mule kept climbing the lone mountain, got on a hogback, dipped into a box canyon, climbed up again — and then seemed to disappear through a cliff. When the prospectors got to where the mule was last seen, they found a trail leading behind a boulder into a natural door through the cliff. This "secret" door opened into a "park." Across the "park" went the mule, passing a great number of elk horns, through another door, into another park. Then down in a gulch the mule began to paw in the sand. The hole it made soon began filling with water. A short distance up the gulch, water was running. Here the prospectors made camp.

This was exactly the kind of place the Apaches would know about, and Baxter and his pardner were very cautious. Against an overshelving cliff they built a semicircular barricade of rocks within which to cook

and sleep. Driftwood caught in crevices between boulders away up the sides of the canyon walls showed
how flood water sometimes raged. It was August, too —
the season of storms. About two o'clock in the morning the Mexican mule stuck his head over the barricade
as if to say, "Be on the watch." The men went back
to sleep. Before daybreak they were awakened by a
turkey gobble. But who ever heard a wild turkey gobble
in August? There was no moon, and light clouds veiled
the stars. Under cover of darkness the men gathered
more boulders to raise the height of the barricade.

With the first light the swish of an arrow through
the air betrayed the turkey. The siege was on. It lasted
all day. John Adair got an arrow in the foot, crippling
him severely. Of course the Apaches had taken possession of the mules. Towards sundown thunder and
lightning began to come out of gathering black clouds.
The intermittent calls of the enemies kept up. With
darkness came rain. A cloudburst threatened.

The pardners decided that their only chance was
up the canyon. If necessary, they could climb the walls
to avoid high water. The way down the canyon was
too exposed. Taking a few provisions and their guns,
they awaited a dark moment, following a prolonged
display of lightning, to start. They had skulked some
distance when the Mexican mule came rushing up,

dragging an Apache lariat. He was a Godsend to the crippled man; both mounted him and rode. Soon the canyon opened into a little valley. Then came the discovery.

As Baxter afterwards told the story, "By the lightning flashes we made out an old partly-burned log cabin across the valley from us, but not far away at that. Close to it was what looked like a sluice box, and it wasn't hard to identify some white bones. Judging from whoops and catcalls in the air, the Indians had discovered our escape. Whippoorwill calls and coyote barks could be heard in all directions except on up the canyon. It wasn't any time to make a thorough examination of the ruins."

The prospectors got out and reached a settlement. Eight years passed before Baxter, accompanied by two other men, went back to examine the cabin ruins and pan the canyon sands. Baxter was a thorough man of the camp; not once did he hesitate on his course.

Jimmie McKenna, one of the prospectors with him, concludes the story: "As we climbed up the lone mountain, Baxter rode ahead to look for the hidden opening into the park. When we came up, we found him staring around him like one in a daze. The whole mountain looked as if it had been crushed by giant hands, as a child would crush a snowball. Not a sign of a tree or of an animal could be seen in any direction. Instead of the park we came into a barren gulch filled with rocks and debris. No water. No vegetation. No animals. No mineral. Nowhere was there a spot smooth enough to camp on. The little valley openings in the canyon were all torn up and filled up with giant boulders.

" 'Boys,' said Baxter, 'we've sure come to the Lost Canyon Diggings. But there'll never be another yellow nugget found here unless another earthquake and cloudburst combined clean out the gulch they filled up. It's death from thirst to hang around here; so we'd better pull our freight for the Mogollons and prospect in them the rest of the summer. Next spring we can come back with a better outfit and see if anything has turned up.' " [1]

Who knows? If anybody knows, it must be the Indian.

[1] Quoted by permission of the publishers, Wilson Erickson, Inc., New York, from JAMES A. McKENNA, *Black Range Tales* (1936), pages 62–63.

IX · The Indian's Secret

"You see, a long time ago, when the 'Paches were thick about here, they used to bring in gold to sell — coarse gold, big as rice, nearly. Never would tell where they got it; but when they wanted anything right bad they was right there with the stuff: coarse gold. All sorts of men tried all sorts of ways to find out where it came from. No go."

"Indians are mighty curious about gold," said Charlie. "Over in the Fort Stanton country, the Mescaleros used to bring in gold that same way — only it was fine gold, there. Along about 1880, Llewellyn, he was the agent; and Steve Utter, chief of police; and Dave Easton, he was chief clerk; and Dave Pelman and Dave Sutherland — three Daves — and old Pat Coghlan — them six, they yammered away at one old buck till at last he agreed to show them. He was to get a four-horse team, harness and wagon, and his pick of stuff from the commissary to load up the wagon with. They was to go by night, and no other Indian was ever to know who told 'em, before or after — though how he proposed to account for that wagon-load of plunder I don't know.

The Indian's Secret

"Well, they started from the agency soon after midnight. They had to go downstream about a quarter, round a fishhook bend, on account of a mess of wire fence; and then they turned up through a *ciénaga* on a corduroy road, sort of a lane cut straight through the swamp, with the tules — cat-tail flags, you know — eight or ten feet high on each side. They was going single file, mighty quiet, Mister Mescalero-man in the lead. They heard just a little faint stir in the tules, and a sound like bees humming. Mister Redskin he keels over, shot full of arrows. Not one leaf moving in the tules; all mighty still; they could hear the Injun pumping up blood, glug — glup — glug! The white men went back home pretty punctual. Come daylight they go back, police and everything. There lays their guide with nine arrows through his midst. And that was the end of him.

"But that wasn't the end of the gobbling gold. Fifteen years after, Pat Coghlan and Dave Sutherland — the others having passed on or away, up, down, across or between — they throwed in with a lad called Durbin or something, and between them they honey-swoggled an old Mescalero named Falling Pine, and led him astray. It took nigh two months, but they made a fetch of it. Old Falling Pine, he allowed to lead 'em to the gold.

Apache Gold and Yaqui Silver

"Now as the years passed slowly by, Lorena, the Mescaleros had got quite some civilized; this old rooster, he held out for two thousand plunks, half in his grimy clutch, half on delivery. He got it. And they left Tularosa, eighteen miles below the agency, and ten miles off the reservation, about nine o'clock of a fine Saturday night.

"Well, sir, four miles above Tularosa the wagon road drops off the mesa down to a little swale between a sandstone cliff and Tularosa Creek. They turned a corner, and there was nine big bucks, wrapped up in blankets, heads and all! There wasn't no arrows, and there wasn't nothing said. Not a word. Those nine bucks moved up beside Falling Pine, real slow, one at a time. Each one leaned close, pulled up a flap of the blanket, and looked old Falling Pine in the eye, nose to nose. Then he wrapped his blanket back over his face and faded away. That was all.

"It was a great plenty. The plot thinned right there. Falling Pine, he handed back that thousand dollars advance money, like it was hot, and he beat it for Tularosa. They wanted him to try again, to tell 'em where the stuff was, anyhow; they doubled the price on him. He said no — not — *nunca* — never! He added that he was going to lead a better life from then on, and wouldn't they please hush? And what I say unt

The Indian's Secret

you is this: How did them Indians know — hey?"[1]

The tale is hoary with age, but by no means decrepit. It still walks, head up. It runs; it can even fly. It has many forms.

Some years ago a hunter after deer worked his way far into the Sandia Mountains. In an especially rough region, remote from any trail, he thought he saw the glisten of sunlight on the prong of an antler in some bushes. Keeping his eye on the spot, he was working towards a better view when a foot went down into nothing. Before he could recover his balance he was at the bottom of a hole with sides and top too smooth to grasp. He was not seriously injured, having fallen not more than ten feet, but the hole was so straight down that he could not possibly crawl out. He found himself in a low-ceilinged cavern of undiscoverable dimensions. The only sign of timber in it was some chips of pine bark. He hoped to dislodge rocks and build a mound to climb out on, but no boulders of any kind were graspable. He explored the cavern darkness, using his matches for light until they were almost all used up. Then he made torches with strips of his clothes. He was hunting for rocks.

Back on a kind of shelf he found something he was

[1] Quoted by permission of the publishers, Houghton Mifflin Company, Boston, Mass., from *Stepsons of Light* (1921), by EUGENE MANLOVE RHODES, pages 82–86.

not looking for. He found some bars of gold. They filled him with joy. He forgot all about his imprisonment — for a while. But he must still get out, to enjoy the gold. He had no water, and the cries for help he sent up into the vast emptiness merely increased his thirst. The cries echoed in the cavern, but he could hear no reverberation against the mountainsides. He shot his gun, which had fallen with him. Night came, and in fits of sleep he dreamed of water and he dreamed of death from thirst. By morning he would have traded half the gold bars for one pine pole. Now, hoping that some other hunter might possibly stalk into hearing distance, he resolved to fire the gun every half hour by his watch, no oftener, until help came or until the cartridges were all expended. He could no longer yell for help. By noon he would have traded all the gold bars off for a pine pole. The shadow in the cavern as well as his watch told him that the sun was far down in the west. He had only three cartridges left and it was almost time to fire again. He was debating over saving these last shots until tomorrow when he heard a voice above him.

The face of a Sandia Pueblo Indian was peering into the hole. "I will let down a pine pole for you to crawl out on," the Indian said.

He was not gone a great while. He returned with a

pole that had notches cut in it and that had evidently been used before.

The hunter came up and drank from the Indian's canteen-shaped *olla*. "For this service," he said to the Indian, "I will now go back and bring you a bar of gold. You shall have the first bar I bring up."

"You find the gold?" the Indian, startled, asked.

"Yes."

The Indian was silent a long time. He seemed to be studying what to say or do. "That gold is for Montezuma when he come back," the Indian finally said. He had his gun in his hand.

The hunter began to try to reason with the Indian. He cajoled, he made many promises. He was afraid to threaten, and he could not attack. The Indian was adamant and he was unceasingly alert. No explanation of the gold would he give, only, "It is for Montezuma when he come back."

The hunter began to feel that if he had mentioned the gold while he was still below, no pole would ever have been let down to him.

At last the Indian said, "I will lead you out, but first the blindfold will go over your eyes and you will give your gun to me."

There was no alternative. It was after dark when the Indian removed the blindfold and the hunter found his feet on a trail. Again and again he went back into the Sandias. He thought he could go to the place where he stumbled into the hole. He thought he did go to the place, but never a hole was there to be found. Whenever he went, always he felt himself watched.

Even liberally granting the fact of the gold bars down in the hole, how can such Indian attitude be credited, now that the Indians are all being educated? Now that the wild Indians, to use the exact Spanish term, have all been *reducidos?* They have not been reduced below the point of still prizing dearer than life a block of land left to them as their own — much of it still a wild mountain land destined to be untameable forever. They have not been educated out of a feel for the earth, which, if nothing but barren desert, is still good earth. Benedict Arnold was not so bad. He merely plotted a change of political proprietors. He did not plot dislodging a people from their own soil. He did not betray his mother — the earth. He did not, while mouthing about "Progress," drain stinking oil into a quiet marsh so that a country man living beside it could never again catch a mess of fish from its pools or watch lovely birds feed among its reeds. Many Indians might be Benedict Arnolds, but it is doubtful if one could be found who would sell away the earth-right of his own people. Certainly, book-educated or merely nature-educated, Indians are no longer so simple as to regard native gold as solely "the white man's money." They still realize, however, what their ancestors learned many generations ago: that the inevitable result of the discovery of gold is the usurpation by white men and machinery of the land containing it.

All this granted, do they have secret knowledge of where the white man's money "grows"?

I am in the trading post at Noschitde of the Navajos. The only Indian within has been standing in one place a long while, not saying a word, looking at I know not what. At last, treading on his soft moccasins, he passes out.

"Did you notice that Indian?" the trader, Charles Newcomb, asks. This trader knows the insides of Indians as well as their blankets and silver bracelets.

"Yes, I noticed."

"That is old Hoseen Nez. He tells me he knows where some gold is in Navajo land. No, he will not show it. He will not get it out himself. He has covered it up, he says. The young educated Indians? They are still Indians. They want their country for themselves. They don't want the white man. They would not trade their land off for tons of gold."

"Do you believe what this Hoseen Nez says?" I ask.

"I don't know."

Apache Gold and Yaqui Silver

The Newcomb men have been among the Navajos a long, long time.

The boy goatherder of the Zuñis stands or sits today on some cliffy headland, his flock beneath, and there by the hour — marked for him only by the sun and the action of bird or rabbit — gazes into distances beyond mountains "a look and a half away." Away to the north, a Navajo sheepherder, perhaps a girl who has studied domestic science in school but in whose screenless hogan there is not even a fly-swatter, is on a butte unseen, the sheep in plain view of whoever passes by; she is looking and looking past the farthest dust-devil whirling on the rim of red desert. Hundreds of miles away an Apache rider mounts to some high point whereon a broken circle of burned rocks tells that his ancestors there sent up signal smokes. Dismounting so that his horse remains hidden behind a boulder, he leans against the weathered rock, blending into it as a rusty lizard blends into the trunk of an oak. Gazing out, he locates one, two . . . six *caballadas* of paint ponies scattered wide apart on the far-stretched, broken basin below. Beyond them, beyond the basin, he gazes until the shadows fall. Not purposely spying against enemies or interlopers, these sentinel-natured gazers keep watch as instinctively as the eagle watches from his skyey pin-

nacle, or as the buzzard, — more eagle-eyed than the eagle itself, — soaring on motionless wings a mile high, awaits the will of God in a fallen sparrow. Each of the Indian gazers sights any hunter or prospector who enters the land, sights the buck deer that the moving hunter is after but misses glimpsing.

Does the watcher see the gold the trespassing prospector is after, the gold in a canyon that is as familiar to him as its runway through a nest of cholla spines is to a pack rat? Let the white man question the Indian. The Indian says nothing. Let the white man look into the Indian's eyes to read the answer. The eyes will look beyond the questioner's like a trapped coyote's. The questioner cannot see what the brain back of those eyes holds.

Wily old Geronimo, while a prisoner at Fort Sill, prompted no doubt by questioners and by his shrewd knowledge of what white men want most, used to talk about gold nuggets in the Guadalupes and in the *mala tierra* — the malpais. He admitted that a party of prospectors once found the gold in the *mala tierra* but said they were all killed before they could get out with their findings. He spoke of how his people covered up showings of ore so as to keep the white man from finding it and ruining the land. For his liberty he offered to guide more than one man to the gold. Geronimo had no use for gold. He would have given all the gold in the world for one more day of the old wild life. Geronimo was a notorious liar. Was he lying about the nuggets? Geronimo was a true Apache.

The Guadalupe Mountains run over into Texas from New Mexico. Not even the most eccentric of hunters for the Lost Adams gold has located it in the Guadalupes, but the Apaches knew these mountains well. Here was one of their last strongholds. If it could be proven that Geronimo was telling the truth about gold in the Guadalupes, then his story of Adams gold would certainly carry more weight.

In San Antonio, Texas, there is a chiropractor who dreams every night of what he will take his oath on any day. He thinks it not only possible but probable that the Apache tradition of gold in the Guadalupes may be substantiated. This is the story he swears to be true: —

"In 1926 an old Mexican who was pretty much stove up all over and was as deaf as a post came into our office. He gave his name as Policarpo Gonzales — called 'Poly' for short. He was as swarthy as old saddle-leather and seemed as out of place in a city as a wild sandhill crane dropped from its winging companions would be in a chicken coop. He spoke good English, and there was a gleam in his eye that caught me.

"All he wanted, he said, was to be able to hear music. We began giving him treatments, and after one about three weeks later, he asked if he could rest a while in the office before going home. While he was resting, some one turned on the radio.

"About that time old Poly gave a whoop, crying out, 'I hear music!' At the same time he began to dance. It was a very peculiar dance, and I asked him where he had learned that style.

" 'From the Apaches,' he answered. His face was gleaming, and when he told us good-by he was swinging his hands and half-humming in rhythm with the music.

"The next day he returned, very grave, moving in a depressed manner. 'Poly, what is wrong?' I asked.

"He motioned me into my private office. There he stood, refusing to be seated, and in tones I shall never forget spoke: 'Doctor, you have done much, very much for me. I hear now the beautiful music. Last night on the plaza I could hear the accordion and the guitar. But I have not money to give you. It is true that I did not promise money, but I owe. I must pay somehow. Listen.

" 'When I was eleven years old my mother gave me to Colonel Boone. That was while he was stationed at Fort Stockton to fight the Apaches. Sometimes I went to school with the children of the officers. Often I rode with the men on scouts. One summer night while only fourteen of us were camped away to the south towards the Chisos Mountains, the Apaches attacked. More than fifty of them there were. They were all yelling. We fought. I know not how many were killed on either side. In the end I found myself wounded in a leg and captured.

" 'Yet I was not afraid. My mother always told me that the blood of the Indian is in my veins. In my heart I am *puro Indio*. The Apaches many times captured Mexican children and trained them to be good Indians. The Apaches were kind enough to me. I learned to shoot the bow and arrow with other boys. I learned their language and to dance.

" 'Also I learned where the Apache gold in the Guadalupes is. The Guadalupe Mountains were our fort. Sometimes I would go into the cave with men and help them break off chunks of the ore. Certain Apaches friendly with the Mexicans who came from New Mexico to catch mustangs or from Chihuahua to haul salt from the salt lake south of the Guadalupes would trade this ore for guns and ammunition. Otherwise there was no use for the gold. There was no regular traffic in the ore, but enough to prove its value. More than one stranger stealing into the Guadalupes to hunt the mine was caught and killed. The Apaches did not want the gold. They wanted to be left alone in their own land. They wanted to keep this land, their home.

" 'All the time the white men kept crowding closer and closer, harder and harder. At last nearly all the warriors in our band had been killed. Some had gone to join Geronimo in Mexico. Then one day the chief called together all who were left and told us that he could hold the land no longer. He told us to fill up the entrance to the cave so as to hide the mine.

" 'It was within reach of a spring. We rolled and carried rocks for days; we covered up all sign of the cave. Then the chief called me to one side. He said I would be back with the white people soon. He and what were left of his people were going to Arizona to surrender, or maybe into the Sierra Madre. He told me if ever I found a white man to trust, I might come back and take gold out of the mine. Soon after that we parted. I was now about eighteen years old.'

"After telling me this, Policarpo walked the floor a few minutes, talking to himself in a language I had never before heard. Then he turned to me abruptly and continued: 'In all these forty-nine years I have been in many places, known many men. Of them all you are the first I have found it in my heart to tell. Anyhow, I owe it to you. If you will take me, I will show you

[138]

where the gold is. If you will dig to it, it will make you rich. Like the Apache, I myself want little.'

"So I went with Policarpo Gonzales. We went to a kind of country that I had no idea existed within the bounds of Texas — a country stark, voiceless, as lonely as it was when the Apaches left it, yet not a desert. We went across rough table-lands into mountains cut by canyons. We left the car at a ranch where we hired horses. Then with a blanket apiece and a few provisions, we rode to the spring which Poly said had been the Indian camping ground. There, in the language of the Apaches, he addressed the departed people and his own departed years, I suppose. 'If I could call them back,' he said to me with tears in his eyes, 'I would be young again.'

"There were plenty of deer in the country, and that night we had venison. Old Poly told me many stories of his youth — stories so definite and circumstantial in detail that there could be no doubt of his having lived with the Apaches, but stories that do not pertain to the mine. In the morning Poly asked that I remain by the spring while he went alone. I remained. That spring is the most natural spring I have ever seen. While I waited, a doe coming to water stopped and looked at me; a javelina emerging from brush wheeled and gave the danger signal to his followers. I had never heard a panther scream, but what I heard across the canyon was, I know, a panther. The wild creatures in the wild land about me made me feel like an intruder. Rightfully it was their country, and I seemed to have no business there. Yet I felt in place.

"When the sun was maybe three hours high, I heard old Poly call. I got up on a high point to see, located him, and obeyed his motion to come to him. A hundred yards away from him I saw his eyes — so clear is the air in the Guadalupes. After I reached him, he led the way down a rough slope. Then he stopped and sat on a rock, gesturing for me to do likewise.

"His voice was pleasant and happy and his face was bright as he said, 'We Indians never forget. I remember everything as well as if it had been yesterday.'

"He was silent a little while. Then he got on his knees, locked his hands together, and put them, knuckles down, on the ground at the point of his knees.

" 'Forty-five feet down, pure gold,' he said.

"He loosened a big rock and showed how the Apaches rolled boulders to fill up the mine entrance. 'When we Indians hide anything,' he said, 'no white man can find it.'

"Of course we were not prepared to excavate forty-five feet of rock. Back at the spring Poly showed me where his lodge and the chief's lodge and other shelters had been. He called the names of some of his playmates. 'Those were the happy days of my life,' he said. Anyone who could have looked into his eyes and heard his voice as I did would have known where a gold mine was.

"We came back to San Antonio, and soon I heard that Policarpo Gonzales had died — 'listening to music.' A year later I made preparations for a long absence and went back to the spring in the Guadalupes and camped for a month. I easily found the spot Poly had located forty-five feet over 'pure gold.' It is marked unmistakably but secretly now. But it takes money to exploit a gold mine seventy miles from a railroad and on private property. There is an old saying that it takes a mine to work a mine. I'm waiting for the mine. I know where the gold is."

While Nat Straw, whose extraordinary career as a grizzly-bear hunter I have told elsewhere, was running sheep in the Navajo country and living with the Navajos, he became close friends with an Indian named Juan. One day Juan told him of a silver ledge so rich that a man could chop the metal out with an axe. "It looks like white iron," he said.

"Show me this white iron," Nat Straw begged.

"For the Navajo who shows it the penalty is death," Juan answered.

"Nobody but you and me will know."

"Yes, the secret would out. I would be killed."

"Then do not show me," Straw concluded, "for I had as soon be killed myself."

A few years passed. It was the spring of 1889. The winter before the snow had lain for one hundred and twenty days on the Plains of San Augustine, where antelopes died like sheep. In one night Nat Straw lost every animal in his herd of thirty-five hundred sheep — and did not have to worry any longer about the snow's keeping the grass covered up. That spring he was in the black sage country south of Pueblos Bonitos, not far from a place where an underground deposit of coal has been burning as long as the Navajo people can remember, the smoke sometimes not being detectable for months at a time and then surging up through fissures of the warped earth so that it is visible for miles.

One day, the subject not having been mentioned at all, Juan said, "We are close to the silver. Nobody will see us. I will show it to you. Be careful, and maybe with it you can gain back a little of your lost fortune."

Juan led the way down into a canyon and back into a cave. He removed some inconspicuous rocks, and there the vein of metal was. Straw took a sample of it

and carried it to a copper mine in the Jemez Mountains
to be assayed. The assay showed nothing but iron,
arsenic and sulphur. The part of the sample not tested
was thrown carelessly to one side.

Not long afterwards some Navajos came to the mine.
They are great hands to look about without seeming to
be prying. They saw that cast away sample of ore.

"Where did this come from?" they asked.

"Nat Straw brought it in," the assayer replied. "It
is worthless." He knew the Navajos knew Nat Straw
well.

They knew the ore also, though they did not tell.
They knew by deduction how Nat Straw had learned
about the ore. Whether they believed the assayer's
estimate of its worth may be doubted. Worthless or
not, a life principle had been violated. They killed Juan.

A squaw warned Straw. He left and has not been
back to the Navajo country since. He went to work,
killing out predatory animals, for the great V Cross T
outfit, on whose range along the Gila River the Navajos used sometimes to come, traveling two hundred
miles, to hunt. One day Nat Straw saw an Indian camp
and went to it. Only two squaws were there. They
recognized him. "Go and not come back," they said.
"Navajo bucks will kill you if they find you." Nat
Straw shifted his trapping to another part of the range.

But back to the Adams Diggings. After spending so many years trailing down the great tradition, what do I think of it? Do I believe the Adams gold ever existed?

If it ever existed, it yet exists. I am cautious. I never have for a minute thought of searching for it myself.

In the plazas along the Canadian River in northern New Mexico, the Spanish-American people — as the Mexicans of that region now call themselves — tell the story of a hunter and his dogs. While this hunter was hoping to kill a bear, he found a rich pocket of placer gold. He was so excited that he let his gun go off accidentally and almost shot away a leg. He tore his undershirt off and with a finger dipped in his own blood wrote on the cotton: "Follow Dogs. I am Dying." Then he wrapped the rag around a nugget of gold — the magnet which draws when pity and Christian charity have no power — and tied it to the collar of one of the dogs and sent them all forth. At last they reached human beings. Unlike the dog of the story book, however, these dogs, although they turned back, could not or would not lead the eager would-be rescuers to their master. That was a long time ago, but the dogs are still roaming the mountains; and sometimes on misty days, when sound carries far, the folk hear them. They call them "Los Perros de la Niebla" — the Dogs of the Mist. And the golden nuggets found by the hunter who wrote his message in blood are known as "The Gold of the Dogs of the Mist."

Is the Adams Diggings likewise but of the Mist? I will finish out Nat Straw's story. He never told me that he went to live with the Navajos and married one of their women for the express purpose of learning the tribal secret of the Adams gold. This I heard elsewhere. Though he told me a lot he learned from the Navajos, he swore he had never looked for the Adams Diggings.

One time while he was prospecting — just prospecting in general, he said — high up in the Mogollons among the mountain tops, he came upon a giant aspen tree. Its smooth whitish bark seemed to ask for carving. He opened his pocket knife and, reaching up above his head, carved a human hand pointing skyward. Then under the hand he engraved these lines: —

THE ADAMS DIGGINGS IS A SHADOWY NAUGHT
AND THEY LIE IN THE VALLEY OF FANCIFUL THOUGHT.

You can prove anything by hearsay evidence. Yet negative proof cannot always disprove a positive. If the Adams gold is a negative, the illusion has at least been magnificently positive. The tradition is a part of the vast land of mountains and silences, of silent people and vistas, of hidden life and hidden death in which

the Lost Adams Diggings still lie lost and still lure on men who dream.

And this dream, based on facts, or based on mere hope, imagination, hallucination, aye, plain fertility in lying — who can say? — this dream will still be a reality long after the mountain trails its questers now follow have been eroded into gullies and the critical infidels of their credulity have gone to dusty oblivion. Guarded by moat, by dynamite, by intricate electric devices as cunning as they are secret, by imponderable tons of bomb-defying cement, and by armed men watched by more watched men, the subterranean vaults of the United States Government at Fort Knox, Kentucky, hold over six billions in golden dust returned to the earth whence toiling miners took it. Not one of the minted coins of this staggering storage has a known story. For all except statistical economists, the mass lies there as inert as a chunk of lead sunk into the fathomless depths of a sunless cavern. It is the gold not yet found that draws and lifts the human spirit. Surely, the root of all evil lies not in the love for this kind of money stuff.

> And the dreamer lives on forever,
> While the toiler dies in a day.

Will the dreamers keep on looking for the Lost Adams Diggings? In Mesopotamia today they are still digging for the treasure of King Nebuchadnezzar of great Babylon, that looter of cities and empires, the same who six hundred years before Christ grazed on grass like an ox and had his naked body wet with the dew of heaven until his hairs were grown like eagles' feathers and his nails like the claws of birds. King Solomon ruled the Jews four hundred years before Nebuchadnezzar looted their treasury. And the dreamers are still looking for King Solomon's Mines. I do not expect the Lost Adams Diggings to be neglected very soon.

Sierra Madre and Bronze Guards

SIERRA MADRE AND
BRONZE GUARDS

There are two Sierra Madres in Mexico: one paralleling the Gulf of Mexico and one the Gulf of California and the Pacific. The Sierra Madre of the Northwest breeds a race of riata rawhide and machete steel.

On the bank of a river in the southern state of Oaxaca, I once saw an old blind cow devouring mangoes that blackbirds were knocking down from two enormous trees and that she was expert in locating by the sound of their fall. Along the trail that led from where Elisha's ravens were thus feeding even a beast, wild plums bent low with red fruit. Only a short distance beyond was the village. As I halted in front of one of the cabins, I saw the owner stir slightly in his hammock, which hung from the roof of the open, earthen-floored *ramada*, or shed. Every habitation in the village had such a shady *ramada*, and every *ramada* was characterized by hanging hammocks. As I walked into the cool shade, a stalwart Indian arose to greet me and offer me a hammock. Then he sank back into his own with these words: "Señor, isn't God good! He gives us the night to sleep in and the day to rest in."

In the Sierra Madre of the North there are no hammocks. The only way the ravens, those "tracks in the sky," ever feed man or beast, there, is to signal out where ferocity has made a kill. Though a man might live there to be older than Methuselah, he would never hear even suggested the soft philosophy of the Oaxacan in his hammock

The Yaqui and the Apache are cousins. The mother of a Yaqui child says to it when it frets: "Be quiet or the *yori* will get you" — not Death, not Devil, not goblins or bugbears, but the *yori* (whites, foreigners). When the child is a little older, she says: "The *yori* killed your father. The *yori* killed your grandfather. The *yori* killed my mother. Son, kill the *yori*. Never trust the *yori*."

Among the fighters whom Don Porfirio Díaz sent to chase the Yaquis was a General Torres. In one battle Torres not only killed many Yaquis but, what was almost unprecedented, captured several alive. Among them was a boy ten or twelve years old; he had been armed. Torres was very anxious to identify a certain chief, but neither he nor any of his men knew this chief except by reputation. Yet it was believed that the chief was among the captives. There were eleven of them, including the boy. The captives would say nothing.

Torres turned to the captain of his firing squad. "Line

them up and shoot every third man. Let the boy stand as Number Twelve. Nits breed lice." Then he added, "God will sort the souls."

"My general," a scout here interposed, "that boy, I am positive, is the chief's son. We can make him talk."

"Wait, then," Torres ordered. Singling out the boy and pointing to the Yaqui warriors, he demanded, "Which one of these men is your father?"

"My father is not here," responded the boy.

"You lie. I know you are lying," Torres flashed back. "You have to tell the truth."

Again came the answer, "My father is not here."

Turning towards his soldiers, Torres ordered, "Hang him up."

Quickly the soldiers placed a rope around the boy's neck, threw it over the limb of a mesquite tree, and pulled him up until he was strangling. Then at a command they lowered him.

"Now, which one of these men is your father?" Torres triumphantly demanded.

"My father is not here," came the answer as calm as it was the first time.

A second time the boy was pulled up. He was held dangling longer and he strangled harder. When he was lowered, the question was put to him with more se-

[153]

verity. He gave his original answer with the original imperturbability.

Torres was in a rage. "You liar," he thundered, "you have but a minute to tell the truth in. This time you will not be lowered."

The boy said not a word.

A minute passed.

"Hang him until he is dead and his soul is in hell," ordered Torres.

The order had barely left the commander's mouth and the soldiers were jerking at the rope, when a warrior sprang forth from the captives. "I am that boy's father," he cried. "I am the chief of the Yaquis you want to kill. You have me."

The rope was slackened. All eyes were fixed on the Yaqui, but he had barely spoken the last word when the boy leaped in front of the general and, with an accusing finger pointed towards the self-proclaimed father and chief, spoke: "He lies. He is not my father. My father is not here."

General Torres ordered the firing squad to action. He had no doubts. God would not have to sort the souls.

Father and son alike belonged to *la raza de bronce que sabe morir*. Of this "bronze race that knows how to die," salute the fiercest defenders of their wild liberty and the most tenacious clingers to their wild land that the continent of North America has spawned — the Yaquis!

Only one man, so far as I know, has witnessed the secret Easter dance of the Yaquis in the Vaca Tete Mountains — not the dances in front of the public at Hermosillo. That man has told me a little of the ceremonies. I may not tell his name. He is a blood brother to the Yaqui. He saved the life of old Puma Blanca from the treachery of a Mexican general. The Yaquis took blood from his arm, took blood from a Yaqui arm also, mixed the bloods in a gourd, and then all drank the mixture. "Your blood is in me," the spokesman of the ceremony said. "My blood is in you. We are blood brothers now."

When the Yaqui warriors invited this blood brother to witness the Easter ceremonials, they told him he must wear *guaraches* (sandals), providing a new pair. The ceremony was at night. It could hardly be called Christian. The Yaquis pay tribute to no priest.

The warriors in the dance wrapped their legs with strings of hollow deer-hoofs in which rattled little round rocks. In the stiff-legged way that only Indians can dance, they began their rhythm. Soon the jerks were rattling the deer-hoofs like a thousand castanets. As a violin string can be rhythmed to shake glass gob-

lets and even, it is said, the tower of a cathedral, so the dancers after a while had the earth under them and the air around them quaking, swaying. While in darkness the earth trembled and the deer-hoofs *click-click-clicked*, the drums of rawhide beat ceaselessly, unendingly, the *tum-tum-tum* of irrevocable inevitability. Then while they danced the dance of doom, the warriors came before the body of the actor representing Pontius Pilate and reviled it, spit upon it, lashed it. The body was not of a man simulating death; it was of a dead man. After the ceremony, the masks of the actors, made of the hide of the javelina (the Mexican musk hog) were burned and the body of the dead Pontius Pilate was removed.

Was the corpse Indian? Mexican? What process of tribal law provides the body? Ask the Yaqui. Ask him also where he got the pellets of gold with which a runner crossed into Arizona to purchase a rifle and ammunition smuggled back into the mountains. These are the Yaquis who guard secrets.

In their Sonoran desert is an immense ant — black, voracious, venomous. When he stings you, you feel a hatpin jabbing to the bone, and the poison makes you faint and sick all over. Not for enemies in war is the ant; he is reserved for traitors, for wrongers of the Yaqui people, for betrayers of the tribe. A man — a

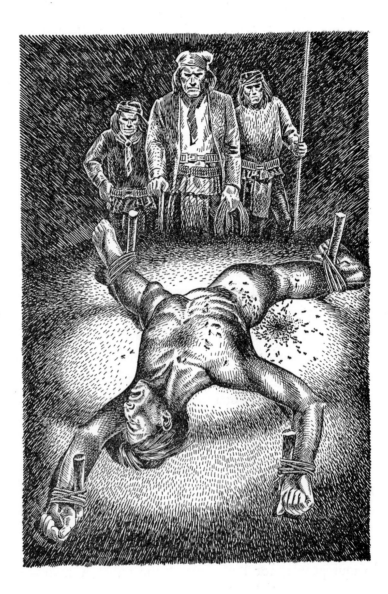

Sierra Madre and Bronze Guards

Mexican *yori*, let us say — is stripped naked and spread-eagled over an ant bed. The ants work at night as well as by day. If the naked *yori* is tied out over the ant-bed when the sun goes down, by the time it comes up only the gristle ligaments fastening his bones together and the cream-yellow bones — soon to become glistening white — will be left. After a dozen or so of the ants have stung a man, he is probably anesthetized for the remainder of the operation.

If there are no ants, there is the sea sand ribbed by the tides of the Gulf of California. The tide rises high on that shore. It comes up lapping, lapping, edging in, receding, but all the time rising, rising. The victim is pinioned so that he can see the sun-silvered breakers coming nearer and nearer and so that his eyes and mouth will be the last part submerged. A few swallows of the salt water will be his last drink, but he can be a long time expecting them. That night he will not see the phosphorescence on the breakers, bright enough for one evanescent moment to line the sights of a rifle by.

If there are no ants or tides, there is always the sun. With his eyelids cleanly cut off and his head fixed so that the Sonora sun glares into his staring eyes, it, white hot and blazing out of a cloudless sky, must soon grow black. Less torturing is a green cowhide wrapped and tied around a victim placed in the sun to wait until the unyielding constriction that rawhide is capable of cuts into muscles and body and finally strangles the very insides to death.

Not many Yaquis living have practised these tortures, but they are a tradition with that people. The Yaquis when well-treated make the best of miners and irrigation farmers. Their valley lands have been taken from them and most of them have come under the rod, but they are still Yaquis. They belong to their *tierra*, their land, more than it belongs to them. They will not betray it. They will not betray its treasure to the *yori*. They can wait and wait, and withhold and withhold.

In higher, moister and better-timbered mountains overlooking the harsh sierras of the Yaquis, live the Tarahumares. They were long ago "reduced," but they also belong to "the race of bronze that knows how to die" — and how to withhold. The first mine the Spaniards opened in their land, Chihuahua, was the Santa Barbara. Here in the seventeenth century the Tarahumares under the leadership of El Hachero killed priests as well as soldiers. Out of the mouth of one dead priest, an old manuscript tells, a white dove was seen to emerge and fly upwards. Certain Indians said the priest was *pariendo* — giving birth; but the Spaniards corrected them, saying that the dove was the priest's soul winging its way to heaven. After this wonder and after a decisive defeat in battle that soon followed, the Tarahumares agreed to submit to baptism — all but El Hachero. He saw his tribesmen baptized; still he refused. "Be baptized or hang," the Christians told him. He did not argue but remained adamant. After the lifeless body had been hacked by the converted Tarahumares until it was "a single wound," and all the hackers had gone away, his wife Tiporaca remained alone by it mourning.

Of the obstinate Ópatas, only scattered remnants and diluted blood now remain, but the Ópatas belong to the Sierra Madre of the North, and their memories run back to times when their ancestors were slaves in mines. Before the "reducement," a force of Spaniards and Spanish allies severely defeated the most formidable opposition the Ópatas could muster. With not an arrow left in their quivers, they withdrew to the edge of a cliff overlooking a profound gorge. The victors sent a messenger demanding surrender. The Ópatas agreed on one condition. This condition the Spaniards refused and began to advance. As the enemy neared, the Ópatas with a shout leaped to their deaths among the rocks hundreds of feet below. Not one remained alive. The crest from which they made their sacrifice is still known as Cerro del Sacrificio.

Apache Gold and Yaqui Silver

An hacienda called Llano Colorado, in Sonora, has been in possession of the Anaya family since 1539. As far back as memory runs, Ópata Indians have lived on the hacienda, among them a family named Navarro. During the centuries mines have been opened, exploited, abandoned in the region. The Ópata folk have seen these things and gone their own way. A scion of the long line of owners of the hacienda, a practicer of international law in Mexico City, told me this story: —

"With us the tradition of a rich deposit of gold on our lands is very old, and the tradition that the Navarro Opatas know where it is equally old. As the region is a proven gold-bearing field, there is nothing extraordinary about the belief; but the tenacity with which the Ópatas keep their secret is remarkable.

"Many years ago a peon on the ranch told Domingo Navarro that he was going to Minas Prietas.

" 'Why?' asked the Ópata. 'You have no money to buy clothes, sugar and coffee.'

" 'That is true.'

" 'Then wait three days and maybe I can help you.'

"The peon told my father of the conversation, and my father put him to watch Domingo. That night Domingo left. The next day the Mexican returned from the trail. He said that he had followed the Indian to the Cerro de Chivato, but that there all sign had disappeared. Two days later Domingo came in with gold valued at between two and three hundred pesos.

"My family educated one of these Indians named Luís Navarro. On more than one occasion I have seen in his possession as much as half a pound of almost pure gold ore, the 'wires' in it visible. Time and again when I have been alone with this man I have tried to get him to reveal the secret mine. 'You are no longer a savage Indian,' I have said to him. 'You are a civilized man. You know how wealth can enrich the lives of human beings. Why don't you denounce the mine and work it?'

" 'No se puede' ('It can't be done') was always the only answer.

"I have offered to buy the gold at market price, but never would Luís sell it to me. He or some of his kin will now and then take a little of the gold to town, turn it over to a saloonkeeper, drink and treat until the saloonkeeper says to quit. Then it is adiós and back to the sierras.

"We have looked and looked for the mine. We think it is in the Mavillo Mountains about twenty-five miles southwest of Llano Colorado. In these severe mountains there is a true oasis: water, trees, fruits, grass, game. Here grow the only bananas I know of in Sonora, along with quinces, peaches, oranges, pomegranates — fruits set out by Spaniards so long ago that nobody knows when. Nobody lives in this place now; deer, jaguars, panthers, and other wild animals have it. About the wilderness garden are the ruins of a rock fence and also of a *vaso* in which ore was smelted. But the dump of slag is a long way off from the *vaso*. Labor cost the Spanish miners nothing, and they often had the Indians to carry slag away on their backs from the smelting place. Perhaps that is the reason the Ópatas will not tell today. Their ancestors were the slaves."

No prospector can ever know the sierras as the Indian knows them — every tree, grass plot, rock, crevice, canyon cut, every wet weather seep and dry weather pot-hole of water, every deer trail and eagle eyrie. His knowledge of secret mines and hidden veins of mineral is traditional; also his chariness in parting with that knowledge. Furthermore, that a fact is traditional does not make it less a fact. The reasons for the Indian's secretiveness are historical.

"My people have a disease of the heart that only gold can cure," said Cortés to emissaries of the Aztec emperor. When the Spaniards reached Mexico City, they saw in the market place Indians from the mountains with "gold dust sealed in quills." When they penetrated to the treasure chamber of the imperial palace, "they saw such a number of jewels and slabs and plates of gold and jadeite ornaments, they were as-

tounded." And, continues the great chronicler Bernal Díaz, who was with Cortés, "I take it for certain there could not be such another store of wealth in the whole world." The store was later valued at seven-and-one-half million dollars.

The mountains whence it came held billions more. The Spaniards had but one desire — to grasp it. They were good prospectors but better miners, and a large portion, probably a majority, of their mineral locations were made through Indian guidance. But when the Indians found their reward for guidance was enslavement to work underground in the very mines they had revealed, they quit telling what they knew. It was probably not the owners of mines who formulated the old Mexican adage: "The poor discover them, the simple work them, and the rich profit by them." When the Indian quit telling, he did not necessarily quit knowing.

His inherited religion and the Christian religion grafted upon that further combined to enforce his secrecy. "The belief that the mountains are the masters of all riches," says Carl Lumholtz in his monumental work, *Unknown Mexico*, "is common among the tribes of the Sierra Madre." Tribesmen may bargain with a mountain for something the mountain is master of, but they cannot bargain with a stranger to show him that something. This belief probably became a part of the Indian's religion after the Conquest. At the same time the Jesuits, in Christianizing the Indians, taught them that if they showed precious metal to anybody but the representatives of God — the Jesuits themselves — God would be angry and take vengeance. The profane must not "steal gold out of God's pocket."

Harold Cobb has made a comfortable fortune mining at Guanacevi, Durango. He knows how to get along with the people. One time, he told me, a Mexican who was freighting ore for him on burros brought in a sample of rock that assayed very rich. Cobb offered to develop the mine for half the profits if the man would show where he had found the sample.

"*Patrón*," the Mexican said, "I am just an *arriero*; I am not a miner. For six burros I'll show you the place and you can do what you will with it."

The agreement was made. The man went off, promising to return soon. A month later Cobb sent for him.

"Well, will you furnish *aparajos* for the burros?" the Mexican asked.

"Yes."

"Then I will come Sunday and guide you to the place."

Another month or so went by and Cobb saw the man again.

"When are you going to show me that mine?" he asked.

"*Patrón*, I have decided that I had rather have mules than burros. Will you give six mules with *aparajos?*"

"Yes," Cobb agreed. "Now let's go, right now."

The man hesitated. "*Patrón*," he finally said, "I'm married to a Tarahumare woman. She says that if I show you the mine I'll die in a year. I don't want to die."

And the *arriero* never did show his vein.

[167]

Apache Gold and Yaqui Silver

A certain *ranchero* had for years kept a Mayo Indian man and woman as servants. One day the man brought in a burro load of bunch grass, pulled up by the roots, and unloaded it in the patio. That night it rained. The next morning the Indian shook the wet dirt out of the roots, fed the grass to the stock, and went off to bring in two mule loads of wood.

Hours later the *ranchero*, while walking about the patio, which the sun had thoroughly dried, saw something shining in the sand. Looking more closely, he found numerous particles of silver. He deduced immediately that they had been brought in on the grass roots. He was so impatient to find out where the grass had come from that he asked the Indian woman. She did not know, but she discovered the master's reason for asking.

When the Mayo came in, he brought a few more bunches of grass along with the wood.

"Where did you get this grass?" the *ranchero* asked.

"In the sierra."

"But in what place?"

"Why, near where I got the wood."

"And the grass you brought yesterday?"

"From the sierra also."

"In the morning we will go get more grass."

"As you order."

But when the *ranchero* got up next morning, the Indians were gone. They did not come back.

The Indian's least concern is in advancing his condition. However, for the sake of friendship or as a return for some favor, he may at times contrive to show something. A case is extracted from the records of the far famed Batopilas Mine in southern Chihuahua, whence have been taken multiplied millions in silver.

About 1850 there came to Batopilas a woman called Doña Natividad Ortiz, "astute, masculine, enterprising and entirely regardless of public opinion. She had been brought up in the Indian country, and knew the language, customs and nature of the Tarahumares." At the time she arrived in Batopilas, there was living in the valley a young Tarahumare named Avila. He was lazy. Whenever it was possible, he was drunk. But he had powers of observation and a native intelligence that singled him out from all other Tarahumares ever known on the Batopilas River. He had worked much in the mines.

Now the señora Ortiz had occasion to favor this Avila, and he began working for her. In a comparatively short time he had located for her three veins in silver. From one of them, Las Ánimas, she took out over three hundred thousands of pesos in silver, living all the while in a cave near at hand, "where she received her friends, celebrated her good fortune, and committed all kinds of extravagancies."

Avila was not forgotten. He did not have to work now. People tried to learn his secret of discovering the hidden metal. "The mulatress does not sleep alone," he might say. The *mulata* is a little surface rock containing oxide of iron and is supposed to keep close to gold or silver. If some spy found Avila sitting alone under a bush smoking a cigarette, he would upon being questioned say that he located silver by tasting it in his tobacco smoke.

Billy Brooks spent thirty-five years prospecting in the Sierra Madre, always with an eye open for the Lost Tayopa Mine.

"One time," he used to tell, "while I was with the Tarahumare Indians, I got wind that my best friend among them — and he was a true friend — knew where a mine was. I tried to hire him to show it to me, but he was like a stump. I tried to impress upon him the advantage it would be to his people if a mine were opened up in the vicinity — how they would make good money working, how their corn would command a good price, and so forth. The Tarahumares seldom use money, they are not looking for work, and they never raise enough corn to last through a season, but finally the Indian relented.

" 'I will not show you the mine,' he said, 'but listen. My calf will show it to you. You stay here in the house. The calf will go to the mine and there I will stake it with a rope. You follow the calf's trail. I myself will not make a trail. You must not see which way the calf goes out with me. You sit here by the fire with your head down. My woman will watch you.'

"For a long time," Brooks said, "I sat by the fire, my head between my hands, the woman watching me. At length the Indian returned.

" 'Follow the calf,' he said.

"I had no idea which way to strike out. So I made a circle cutting for sign. I found some disturbed rocks indicating where the calf had set back on its rope and been dragged. I followed the calf tracks. At some places the Indian had driven it instead of leading it and the tracks were hardly visible. It took me hours to work the trail out.

"Along late in the day, however, I came upon an old hole over the edge of which I saw a rope hanging. One end of the rope was tied to a bush not far from the hole. I looked down. There the calf was on the other end of the rope, choked to death. It had evidently stumbled into the hole and hanged itself. I pulled it out,

[171]

removed its entrails — for it was good to eat — and returned to the Indian's camp. I told him what had happened.

" 'Thus it is, thus it is!' he exclaimed, very well satisfied. 'I knew that calf would die if he showed you the mine. If I show you, then I die too. How I die, I do not know, but somehow.'

"The Indian's mine had a vein of ore all right, but it was not worth working."

This is not a book of documented facts; nevertheless, it is a history. It is a history of what men have believed in — not creeds, but luck, fortune through chance, the fulfillment of hope. What men believe or fancy to be true, what they have faith in, whether phantom or fact, propels their actions. The hunter of precious metals is always a fatalist, no matter how civilized above superstition he may be. Deep in his heart he believes that somewhere out in the sierras the magic scales are awaiting him.

Long ago, as the story goes, a poor Spaniard by the name of Quintana, who had once been rich but who had lost everything, lived in the city of Tepic. To keep his family in *tortillas* and beans he had to toil like a peon, but he was proud and, like an eagle in a cage, he kept looking for a way to rise.

Now on a certain feast day while all the world, as it seemed to this Spaniard, was free from toil and only he must work, he was with heavy feet walking towards his drudgery when he happened to notice a certain shop facing the Plaza de Armes. It was a jewelry shop called "The Foot of Venus," and its window was full of finery. But, among all the rings and chains of gold, the bracelets of silver, and the sparkling stones, the one thing that caught his attention was an ordinary pair of scales for weighing gold. He had seen other such instruments, many of them; but this one fascinated him in a peculiar way.

He stood for a long time gazing at it. He counted the tiny weights piled by its side and began estimating the amounts of gold they would balance. In imagination he saw piling up back of the scales heaps of gold that in future years would be weighed upon the delicate instrument — gold that would buy everything fine in the world — fine houses, fine clothes, images of carved ebony, carriages, liveried peons, all the things he would like to have. Then somehow it seemed to him that if he could but possess the scales, the gold appropriate to their purposes would come to him. He had to tear himself away from the window and hurry on to his work, but all day his head was awhirl with the vision of gold. He forgot his present poverty; he was living in future magnificence.

If only he could possess the scales! He must possess them! Somehow he would possess them. An ambition that seemed realizable burned in his breast. It gave him new hope and energy. The despondency, the rebellion against circumstances, and the futile nursing of a ragged pride that had been eating away his soul left him. He determined to work harder than he had ever worked, to save penny by penny, and to buy the scales. On his way home that night he stopped again in front of The Foot of Venus and looked at the little instrument. When he told his wife, though, of his plan, she was a veritable wet-blanket.

"You," she said — "what on earth would you do with the scales even if you had them? Will you take *tortillas* from the mouths of your children to buy a plaything for your own fancy? This notion will make your head as soft as the yellow of an egg."

"Yes," answered the Spaniard, "or as hard as the head of a burro. I admit that I do not know exactly what I shall do with the scales, but they have cast a spell over me. I am determined to have them. It is useless to oppose the will of God. Something inside me says this little machine will make our fortune."

Quintana did not starve his children, but he almost starved himself. Not one *cigarro* did he smoke, not one swallow of *pulque* drink. Each week he tied up a little coin in a piece of buckskin, and every day he counted the coins like a miser. He had but one fear; that was lest the scales be sold before he accumulated enough money to buy them. No other scales but these would do. Twice each day with a smothered feeling he approached the shop, and always he saw the scales in their place unsold. After many months he had enough money to buy them.

Possession seemed to advance his ideas. He bore the instrument proudly to the owner of a small vacant shop in a street down which Indians came from the mountains.

"Señor," he said to the landlord, "I want to rent your shop. I have no money to pay rent, but these scales for weighing gold will make money for me and you too, if you will only afford me a place to house them."

"What are you to stock the shop with?" the landlord asked.

"This and this only," replied the owner of the little

[175]

instrument, balancing it. "And I need nothing else, for it will bring money to itself."

"Well," said the landlord, "take the shop and keep the scorpions out of it until I can find a paying tenant."

So Quintana set up his scales in the shop. He could not be there all day, for he continued to work and also to save; but for an hour every morning before his task-work began, and every evening after his task-work was done, he sat in the shop. Meanwhile he was accumulating another collection of coins in the buckskin.

One evening an Indian who was passing by looked through the open door, saw the scales, and stopped. "Do you buy gold, sir?" he asked.

"That is my business," Quintana answered.

The Indian produced some yellow dust. Quintana weighed it and offered in exchange something over half the money he possessed. The Indian haggled for more; Quintana squinted at the balances and raised the offer. Finally, by paying every cent he had, he bought the gold. The next day he sold it at a fine profit. Thenceforth he did no more day labor. He sat and waited for Indians to come. They came, bringing gold from no one knew where. That was their secret. The Spaniard bought as cheaply as he could but at a price that kept the Indians satisfied. He grew rich. He bought himself a fine house and had carriages and servants. He dressed his family in fine clothes and had *mole de guajalote* to eat as often as he wanted it.

Yet he was not satisfied. He wanted more. He wanted the mine from which the Indians brought the gold. "If I could only get hold of it," he said, "I should be as rich as the great Borda. I could put up a cathedral like the one he built in Taxco, and I could lay out gardens like his in Cuernavaca. I should be as rich as the Count de Regla." But when he tried to pry their secret from the Indians, they were silent.

He was cunning, however, and he thought of a plan. He was in the good graces of a certain *padre* who had lived among the Indians. To this priest he went. "Father," he said, "these Indians have a gold mine that is of no use to them. They do not know the value of money and they don't need money anyhow. They are barbarians, and it is sheer stubbornness that keeps them from letting others know where the gold lies. By gifts and kindness you can win their confidence. I charge you to do this, and we will divide the riches; half for you and the church, and half for me."

The plan seemed good to the *padre*, and he at once set about winning the secret from the natives. They proved to be exceedingly stubborn. Finally, however, after he had been very generous to them, had protested many times how he loved them, and had argued over and over how as their confessor he should have at least one glimpse of their mine, they agreed to take him — just once — provided he would go blindfolded.

This was a hard provision but the *padre* accepted it. "God has made this a fertile land," he said to himself. "The rainy season is now upon us. I will fill my pockets with corn, drop the grains secretly as I ride along on the burro, and within a few weeks I can trace the path by green shoots of corn."

He started the blindfolded journey from the Indian village. In a much shorter time than he had expected, the blindfold was taken off his eyes. They fell upon a stream of water flowing over a bed of gravel and sand flecked yellow with gold. He was in a narrow, steep canyon to which he felt sure there was only one ingress. The sprouting corn would mark the trail leading into the canyon. The Indians gave him several very fine nuggets, put the blind on him again, and his burro started.

When he reached the village and the blind was once more removed, one of the older Indians handed him a bag, saying, "Father, here is some corn you lost from your pockets on the trail. I gathered it all up for you and you will find not a grain missing."

Sierra Madre and Bronze Guards

Not long after this episode the Spaniard was seen stealthily following some Indians in the mountains. He did not return. What he was after is still in the sierras.

The Jesuit priest has both openly and in disguise returned many times to the Sierra Madre, but he has learned nothing. The Indian remembers a certain lesson, as a certain little tale will tell.

At a Tarahumare pueblo in the Sierra Madre, a long time ago, there used to be a renowned Virgin — an image. She was hollow, and her head screwed down tight on her neck, where it was locked. A cacique, a head man, of the Tarahumares kept the key. Whenever some miracle was desired, the Tarahumares got the cacique to unscrew the head so that they could pour coins, pieces of unminted silver and gold, and precious stones into the Virgin's body. Nothing was ever taken out of her, and naturally in time she grew to be heavy with wealth.

Then the Tarahumares, who were being pushed deeper into the high mountains, decided that they would move the Virgin nearer their habitations, so that her beneficent effect could be realized there. But they could not budge her. She acted as if she were planted.

Much distressed, they went to the priest. He understood the ways, sometimes stubborn, of *santos*. "Let

me have the key to the blessed Virgin's head," he said, "and I will see that she yields to your desire to move her. In the morning go to her and you will find her ready and willing to travel."

He took the key. The night passed. In the morning the Virgin lightly and gladly went with the Indians.

Such are the natives and such are the traditions of their knowledge of silver and gold in the land of Tayopa — the Sierra Madre of the North.

The Lost Tayopa Mine

THE LOST TAYOPA MINE

Tayopa has, I suppose, been the longest sought-for, the most extensively hunted, and the most widely talked-of lost mine in North America. The search that any one man has made for it is but an episode in the Odyssey that generations of adventurers have woven out of accredited history and incredible legend. The story of it, which I have worked far harder to shorten than to spin out, is based on Spanish enterprise that penetrated the wildest lands held by the wildest Indians of the vast empire of Spain. It is bound up with Jesuitical teachings and savage superstitions. It is the depth and mystery of the Sierra Madre of the north and the secret of tribes that seem coeval with the ageless mountains themselves. Barriers of tangled mountains and barrancas, or gorges, that cut as deep as the mountains are high have so isolated the setting that it, like the lost mine itself, seems a story out of another world long vanished. Tayopa is of the buried past; yet it remains the perennial hope of men searching today and laying plans to search tomorrow.

I · Camino Real of Silver Pack Trains

Many men, representing varied nations of the globe, have set out for Tayopa from many directions. Yet for me the one place from which it is oriented will always be the Cerro Miñaca. This hill rises on a plain over-looking the village of Miñaca some two hundred kilo-meters — as the railroad twists — west of Chihuahua City. It takes the tri-weekly train all day to get there, the terminus of rails. Beyond lie the Sierra Madre ranges, towering, barranca-cut, impassable except to footmen, airplanes, burros, and other hardy beasts. The people of the sierras say that the first Spanish *padres* rode through mounted on black oxen.

The main trail — the *camino real*, the "royal road" — across this part of the Sierra Madre has been traveled since the time of the Spanish Conquest; doubtless, In-dians traveled it long before the Spaniards came. It is still a *camino real* — a "royal road," but, though no rail-way or modern highway has supplanted it and perhaps never can supplant it, it is less traveled now than it was two hundred years ago. On some stretches of it a man may ride one, two, or even three days without meeting

[186]

a soul. The through traveler will be on a Spanish mule, accompanied by another mule loaded with bedding and provisions behind which trots a *mozo* — guide and servant — as tireless as the mules.

The trail crosses timbered mesas, the charred stumps of pine torches beside it telling how the running Tarahumares have raced here in the night. It leads down into canyons along which these singular Indians live in smoked caves or in shelters of poles only a little more substantial than the nests of eagles, dress in breechclouts, perform rites to "the diabolic root," *peyote*, and fade from view when a stranger approaches. It winds under mountains on the sides of which, too steep for an ox to walk, the *mestizo* and the pure-blooded Indian alike plant corn by punching holes with a stick in the rock-littered soil, leaving the plants for nature to cultivate. It zigzags down into a little valley where a few wooden-wheeled carts haul grain and wood over trails as limited as the race-track of a slot machine. It enters silent forests in which gunless Pima Indians cut down great pine trees in order to kill a little squirrel. From the mountains overtopping Ocampo, snowclad in wintertime, it pitches down a mile in half a day's ride to the torrid level of oranges growing along the Mayo River and wild-cotton trees with thorn-studded trunks sticking out of its cliffs. Then it corkscrews upward again into

[187]

pine and spruce and the red-hued madroños flagged
with the cocoons of the Mexican silkworm. It prongs off
to pass the spot where bandits left a man buried one night
with his head sticking out of the ground and returned
next morning to find that lobo wolves had guillotined
it. It passes many mounds of rocks, each supporting a

cross, marking places where death has struck or where, on the crests, man and beast have since time immemorial been accustomed to halt for breath. And each time one of the faithful comes to such a marker he will make the sign of the cross and add another rock to the pile. The trail goes through the territory of the now tribeless Ópata Indians, the women of which still weave baskets of the "Rattlesnake in the Grass" design and entwine into fiber *ollos* symbols secret to their people. It goes on into the varied lands of the Yaqui Indians of still unsubdued fierceness.

Whoever follows this trail westward from Miñaca will travel two hundred and fifty miles without seeing a pane of window glass or going through a pasture gate. He may pass the weekly — in flood season perhaps the monthly — mail, which goes only a part of the distance, carried on a little mule driven by a sandaled footman. Along the trail women comb their long black hair with combs made of cactus burr, boys at harvest-time stand on guard to frighten deer and bear out of corn patches, and old men sit up all night smoking javelinas to death in a rocky den.

Yet church bells have been tolling these people to pray for hundreds of years, though more than one agroupment of hovels where a church once stood now has nothing churchly left but an ancient bell, hung

from a pole. Here and there, beyond the sound of any bell, the trail becomes a ladder of little round holes, knee-deep to a burro, that only the hoofs of centuries of climbing mules could have worn in the everlasting rock. The chief freight they carried was supplies into and silver out of the mines. Along these ways *conductas* once bore cargoes of silver bars to be shipped across the Spanish Main. "In those days," says one historian, "iron and steel were worth more than silver, which was often used to shoe mules with."

That was when Tayopa was in bonanza. Probably

Anyway, the records I saw established the fact that, in the seventeenth century, Tayopa was a mining camp of sufficient importance to have its own *cura*. At that time there were probably not three other *curas* in what is now the state of Sonora. If it had a *cura*, it had a church. The church should have been built of stone; if so, remains of it should be evident today. The Apaches were very hostile towards the Spanish in Sonora towards the close of the seventeenth century; my guess is that Tayopa had to be abandoned because of them. I judge it lay somewhere between Nácori Chico and Guaynopa."

As to where Tayopa lay, many judges have made many judgments, based on varying evidence. In 1885 an officer in the United States Army, Britton Davis, while chasing Apaches in Sonora, found in the little town of Nácori "a curious state of affairs. The population was 313 souls; but of these only fifteen were adult males. Every family had lost one or more male members at the hands of the Apache."

Here also, Britton Davis goes on to say in his autobiographical book *The Truth about Geronimo*, "I first heard the legend of Tayopa. This mine was said to have been of such wonderful richness that blocks of silver taken from it had to be cut into several pieces so that mules could carry them to the seacoast for shipment to Spain. My informant, the white-haired *presi-*

dente, a man over eighty years of age, told me that his grandfather, who also had lived to be a very old man, had worked in the mine as a boy, and that it was in a mountain range to the east of Nácori.

"The Apaches attacked the place one day when the men were nearly all away at a *fiesta* in one of the river [Río Bavispe] towns, killed every one in the camp, destroyed the buildings, and blew up the entrance to the mine. A hundred years went by with no force in the country strong enough to conquer the Apaches and the mine has never been found.

"Those who would seek, as have hundreds before them, the lost mine of Tayopa, should bear in mind the statement of the old *presidente's* grandfather: 'Here in Nácori, where we stand, on a still night one could hear dogs bark and the church bell ring in Tayopa.'"

More than one traveler who passed through the state of Chihuahua during the middle quarters of the last century noted the utter abandonment of ranches and settlements on account of Apache devastations, though in Chihuahua City itself the windows of the Governor's Palace were festooned with strings of dried Apache scalps and the plaza in front of the cathedral was ornamented with Apache heads on the tops of poles. These trophies, however, were not brought in by

Mexicans but by a strange assortment of adventurers from the north who scalped for bounty.

Their leader for a time was James Kirker — until he took to collecting bounties on Mexican scalps. In 1842 Kirker, seventy Shawnee warriors under Chief Spiebuck, Captain James Hobbs, and several other scalp hunters set out after a strong band of Apaches that had captured, almost within sight of Chihuahua City, a train of eighty mules bringing freight from Vera Cruz. Only one Mexican escaped the attack. The scalp hunters followed the Apaches for days until, on the western slope of the Sierra Madre, they overtook them.

Here, "close to a lake," says James Hobbs in the book *Wild Life in the Far West*, which he wrote thirty years later, "we found some ancient ruins, the cement walls and foundation stones of a church; and a *lignum vitae* cross, which seemed as sound as it had ever been. We also found remains of a smelting furnace, a great quantity of cinders [slag], and some drops of silver and copper. From the appearance of the ruins, it seemed as if there had been a considerable town there. The lake was the headwaters of the river Yagui [Yaqui]. . . . We left the country with regret. . . . Besides the remains of furnaces, we saw old mine shafts that had been worked, apparently long before. Specimens of gold, silver, and copper ore that we took to the mint at Chihuahua were assayed and pronounced very rich."

Were the scalp hunters at Tayopa? If so, Jim Kirker should have known, though he need not have told. For a time he had lived with the Apaches — and the Apaches knew. No oral testimony concerning Tayopa is more strongly relied upon than that of another "White Apache" named Casimero Streeter.

When Frémont raised the American flag in California in 1846, tradition goes, Casimero Streeter rode from Santa Barbara to join him. Not long afterwards he killed an army officer, was forced to flee, and took up with the Apaches. He raided with them, scalped with them, and was in every way one of them. He was called "the White Apache." A brother of his came to live at Cananea, in northern Sonora, and on one occasion he told this brother that while he was raiding with a band of Apaches to the southeast, warriors pointed out some ruins in a canyon away down below them and said, "That is Tayopa. Leave it alone. Never try to go to it." He said that in the clear air he could distinguish a bell on the church. He gave his brother general directions to the site, locating it on a fork of the Yaqui River, but warned him that he could never take even a strong expedition to it because of the Apaches. Not long after this he was shot at Nacozari, by the brother of a girl he was transporting across the village — with merely courteous intent, it seems — on his horse. His name was preserved by the *banda de Streeter* — "the Streeter gang" — composed of a few renegade Apaches, Yaquis and Mexican bandits, until modern times.

Any logger of the trail to Tayopa learns that every man who has traveled that trail has used a compass of which the needle varies according to the magnetism in the hand of the user.

One day in the year 1910 a Mexican by the name of Marcos Peralta appeared at the Monte Cristo mine operated by the Día Claro Mining Company on a tributary of the Yaqui River in eastern Sonora. He thought he had some information that would interest mining men. He was not mistaken.

According to his story, while he was riding by a ruined house several months before, he heard groans. Halting to investigate, he found a very old man, sick and starved. He took him home and with the help of his wife nursed him to recovery.

When the old man was strong enough to be about, he said, "I can never repay you for your kindness, but I will give you something that may be of value."

Thereupon he untied a buckskin string from his neck and drew out from under his shirt a buckskin bag. He opened the bag and took from it a sheet of dirty, frazzled paper on which, however, the details of a map could still be made out.

"When I was but eighteen years old," the old man explained, "I became caretaker for a church. It was an ancient church, built by the first Spaniards who came into the Sierra Madre. The *padres* were good to me, and one of them taught me to read and write. As soon as I began working in the church, I saw how the balcony was ornamented with wrought silver. Then I learned that more silver — much silver — was concealed in the church vault. I was sworn to secrecy and I kept the secret, but I could not keep from wondering where all this silver came from.

"One day I was cleaning out the chests and cabinets in the sacristy. They were full of records, very old, about births, baptisms, and the like, and because I had learned to read I often stopped to look into them. Then I came to a document different from all the others. It set down so many ingots of gold delivered, so many silver bars delivered. It gave the names of the masters of the pack trains who brought this wealth, also the dates. Also put down was where the metals came from. The place was Tayopa, and there was a clear map to Tayopa.

"I had long heard of Tayopa, the richest mine in the world. The map was a picture of the Yaqui country. Not even the soldiers of Mexico could go in there then. This fact was notable among the most ignorant.

"What I learned I kept to myself and went on with my work. Then the *padre* who had been so good to me died. In his place came a fat beast from Italy. One day while I was cleaning in the balcony I heard a woman cry out. I rushed down. The fat beast left the woman and withdrew. After that he was my enemy. Once I tasted of poison he had dropped into my food. I feared him, and he had something to fear from me. I saw I could no longer continue as *mozo* in the church and live. I decided to copy the map to Tayopa and leave. I copied it with great secrecy and with exactness. You see the copy before you. I have never tried to follow the map, for I have no power and am poor and ignorant. Now the map is yours."

The manager of the Día Claro Mining Company repaired the map, saw that mountain peaks on it were described by degrees of longitude and latitude as well as by altitude and that a route to the mine was marked. The Tayopa tradition was to him, of course, not unfamiliar. He knew that the Phelps Dodge Company, one of the most powerful mining companies in the world, had a prospector at that very time looking for Tayopa. He made up a party of thirty men, mostly Mexicans, and, carrying enough provisions on pack animals to last a month, set out southward for the starting point as given by the map to Tayopa.

Having located this starting point, the expedition entered a country exceedingly rough even for the Sierra Madre. They found themselves following something like an old trail, but their course was determined by measurements from peak to peak according to the map. Gorges and *barrancas* more than once turned them back. Then at last, having passed the ultimate peak called for, they descended into a valley so surrounded by mountains that not even an experienced mountaineer would have guessed its existence before entering it.

Here in this valley they found the outlines of ruined adobe houses, pines three feet in diameter growing out of them. They found between fifteen and twenty shafts that measured some eighty feet in depth, all of them deep in water. Also they found tunnels. Yet no slag or smelter was visible until they dug into a mound. This mound was a great slag pile topped by an overburden of rock and earth four feet deep that had evidently slid down from the mountain above it. Considering the residue of silver left in ore by the primitive processes of extraction, the amount found in the slag was disappointingly low. This lack was soon explained, however, for pillars of earth left to support the roofs of some of the tunnels yielded a mixture of silver and lead that was "self-fluxing." That is, when this native ore was melted, no silver remained. Subsequent analysis of the samples taken showed a yield of from five hundred to twenty-five hundred ounces of silver to the ton.

The leaders of the expedition were satisfied that they had located the lost Tayopa — located it in a lost world, no human being apparently living within a great distance of it, the hidden valley bearing no evidence of having been visited by man during recent times. A property so remote as this, no matter how rich, could be developed only by a well-financed company able to transport machinery over the mountains, pump out the water, and otherwise spend much money. The discoverers returned to Monte Cristo and organized the Cinco de Mayo Mining Company. They raised enough money to denounce the property — to survey it and put up monuments marking the boundaries of the claim. Their intention was to sell out to some powerful company.

In order to maintain title they were by law required to pay taxes and do some work. Meantime the Madero Revolution was sweeping the country. Pancho Villa and other leaders of his kind were tearing up railroads, killing cattle, confiscating all kinds of property. The Día Claro Mining Company withdrew from Monte Cristo, where the organizers of the Cinco de Mayo

Company were employed. They were scattered to the
four winds. The revolution dragged on for years and
years. Taxes lapsed. Some of the men responsible died.
When one of the stockholders told me the story, he
said that he did not know the whereabouts of a single
man who had entered the valley of Tayopa, that he himself had not accompanied the expedition, that he had
no map, and that he doubted if he could go to the
place.

But these Cinco de Mayo men found no ruined
church at their location — and Tayopa must have had a
church.

II · Eight Days Towards the Sunset

Of all the men who have set out on the trail for Tayopa, no one has searched for its record so assiduously as Henry O. Flipper. He was a remarkable character. Last heard of in South America, he is, if still alive, past eighty. A Negro, he graduated from West Point and for a time served as lieutenant in the border country. Then he was dismissed from the army. He was a master of the Spanish language and a student of Spanish-American history and laws. For a time he served as interpreter at Santa Fe, where he wrote a few historical articles. He made a translation of the Mexican mining laws; he compiled Spanish and Mexican land laws. For years he lived in Chihuahua, surveying and investigating records for mining companies. Then, early in this century, he was employed by Bill Greene.

Greene was one of the most spectacular figures that the Southwest ever knew. Under Porfirio Díaz he was granted mineral concessions on three million acres of land in Sonora and Chihuahua. He handled cattle by the tens of thousands. He floated bonds and stocks by the tens of millions. He helped build the Northwestern

Railroad of Chihuahua and at the cost of over $500,000 projected a wagon road to Ocampo that reverted to a mule trail. He controlled mines — gold, silver, copper — in Arizona and the northern states of Mexico and ran timber camps. He was a dreamer, a showman, a flamboyant speculator; he grubstaked every gambler, drunkard, and bum who could reach him with a tale about a mining prospect. It was inevitable that the magnificent Greene should become enthralled by the prospect of Tayopa.

He knew that Flipper had interested himself in the tradition and was familiar with both the Sierra Madre and Spanish mining laws. He sent Flipper to Spain to investigate original sources pertaining to the mine. Had Greene's financial bubble not burst, had the Revolution not come, and had Flipper with ample time and money at his disposal proceeded to search the Sierra Madre for Tayopa, the result might or might not have been another tale of failure. In the end, Flipper from far away South America sent a report of his findings back to another Tayopa seeker in this country.

"The first time I heard of Tayopa," wrote Flipper, "was in 1889. At that date I had not the remotest interest in the subject. I was down in Sonora surveying public lands under a concession held by General Francisco Olivares. One day while I was in Hermosillo working on some maps, a Spaniard came into the office and handed a bulky document to Jesús Santa Cruz, a lawyer engaged by General Olivares. The document lay about the office for several days and all of us read it. It was written on paper of foolscap size and was signed by three priests. Their names were subsequently verified by General Olivares, in Mexico City, as belonging to Jesuits important in early Spanish colonial history. Santa Cruz finally sent out a fruitless expedition to try to locate Tayopa. He is long since dead.

"According to this document, the Tayopa mines at the time of the great Indian uprising of 1646 had not exported any silver for years, though they had been in bonanza from 1632. When the Indians rose up throughout the Sierra Madre, an immense amount of bullion must have been in storage at Tayopa. It is not unlikely that about this time the Jesuit owners, with Indian labor, covered up their mineral workings; all on the grounds may have been killed. Tayopa seems to have fallen in 1646, though some evidence points to a later date.

"The most persistent seekers after Tayopa have been the Jesuits. Long a thorn in the side of Spanish authorities, Spain in 1767 suppressed them and drove them out of Mexico. They had a power over some Indians that no other representatives of the Christian religion have ever been able to gain. They are credited with having charged the Indians, under penalty of an awful curse, never to reveal the location of mineral wealth to any but representatives of the Jesuit Order. In 1909 while I was living in old Jesús María (Ocampo), many Jesuits came into the Sierra Madre, taking charge of churches that had for generations been abandoned and even establishing themselves where there were no churches. In one little Indian village without a church there were four Jesuit priests. The mountain natives thought these Jesuits were after Tayopa and other lost mines or hidden treasures. Whatever they were after, the Revolution of 1910 prevented their accomplishing anything.

"One traditional document — not the one I saw in Santa Cruz's office in Hermosillo — says there was bullion to the amount of 23,000,000 pesos secured in a tunnel or prison vault, the entrance to which was barred by an iron door 2281 varas east and 63 varas south of the door of the church in Tayopa. I never took stock in the bullion story, but to my mind there is no doubt that the Tayopa mines existed.

"The only definite thing that all my researches in Spain netted was a traveling direction. I give it verbatim:

"*On the 7th day of March stand on the summit of*

Eight Days Towards the Sunset

Cerro de la Campana, near the Villa de la Concepción, and look at the sun as it sets. It will be setting directly over Tayopa. Travel eight days from the Cerro de la Campana towards the sunset of March 7th and you will come to Tayopa.

"I have had no opportunity to work on this clue. The only Villa de la Concepción in the state of Chihuahua that I know of is the town known at present as Guerrero. It is a very old place and perhaps the oldest main trail across the Sierra Madre leads to it from the west. Only a few miles south of it is the town of Miñaca. Right out on the plain against Miñaca is a *cerro*, or hill, called Cerro de Miñaca. Long, long ago that *cerro* was called Cerro de la Campana — from its *campana*, or bell, shape. It is a notable landmark for many miles around.

"Of course the latitude of the sunset varies with the seasons, but a man riding west from Miñaca for any considerable distance, no matter at what time of the year, would have to follow the old Sonora Trail. Only an airplane could go in a straight line over the tumbled mountains and awful gorges of the Sierra Madre. The Sonora Trail keeps a general direction. Over some stretches of it a man can ride for a whole day almost without finding a place where he can turn out. Again there are intersecting trails. Towards the boundary line

CERRO DE MIÑACA

of Chihuahua and Sonora the trail makes several distinct prongs.

"A regular day's travel with *mozo* and pack animal in the mountains is twenty-five miles. Often, however, a traveler cannot cover that much distance.

"In consequence of all these facts, the directions for finding Tayopa eight days west from the Cerro de la Campana may not be very helpful. A man will have to explore a vast country before he can use to advantage any map or chart.

Eight Days Towards the Sunset

"God alone knows where Tayopa is. The old line between Chihuahua and Sonora was originally very indeterminate. A considerable strip of what is now Chihuahua was formerly in Sonora. My own opinion is that Tayopa is located somewhere near the Sonora-Chihuahua boundary in the vicinity of Guaynopa, not far from the Río Aros. An old tradition has it that dogs barking in Guaynopa could be heard in Tayopa. . . . But the hunter must look everywhere."

III · Under the Mesa of the Bell-Maker

When I met C. B. Ruggles in 1927, he was armed with the Flipper report just quoted and had already spent six years looking for Tayopa. Before that he had just about run the gamut of outdoor occupations of the West. His father had been a government physician who practised among the Indians of the Northwest and invested his savings in cattle. Ruggles had a smattering of both medicine and surgery, and had known Indians and the mountains all his life. He had ranched, trapped, hunted, mustanged, prospected, and guided parties into the Rocky Mountains before there were roads and trails. Above all, as I found, he was extraordinarily observant and one of the most interesting talkers as well as agreeable human beings I have ever met.

I went to Ruggles to get a story. I got it — and went with him. His own search began when one day a human wreck lurched into his hunter's cabin on the edge of Taos, New Mexico. The stranger was dressed in rags and patched buckskin; he wore nothing on his feet but the rawhide *guarachas* (sandals) of the Mexican peon. After more than thirty years spent in the Sierra Madre, he told, the revolution had run him out. He called himself Burgess, but that was not the name his father and mother bequeathed him. He had two secrets: why he had changed his name and a clue to Tayopa. Ruggles outfitted him to trap and gave him a home. The revolution went on; Burgess died, and Ruggles in 1919 crossed the Rio Grande to work out the trail to Tayopa. He had a considerable amount of money when he started.

He told me of trails he had followed and of trailless regions he had entered; he related experiences he had had — with an ambush of bandits whom he discovered before they discovered him, with a Tarahumare who stole his mules and played a homemade fiddle; with two Pimas who planted in his trail daggers of the maguey leaf tipped with rattlesnake venom that had been caught in a deer's liver; with distrustful natives who at one time set fire to a forest in which he was camped and at another time rolled boulders down a mountain to blockade a narrow pass in front of him; with a Mayo Indian who quit the pursuit of four maverick "Sonora black" cattle to follow him; with a Yaqui who shot at him from a cliff a thousand feet over his head and missed; with javelina hogs that led him into a long abandoned mine tunnel that he for a time took to be Tayopa. He had gone into Mexico while the country was still lawless from the effects of years of revolution. Yet, despite certain experiences, he had found the folk of the sierras friendly and hospitable. Always free with the medicines he carried in his pack, he had won the name of *el doctor* over a wide territory.

But he had not won Tayopa. Once the trail seemed hot when he received authentic information of a church bell with the name TAYOPA cast into it. One of the traditions of Tayopa is that mission bells were cast there. Ruggles traced the bell to Hermosillo, the capital of Sonora, and there found that a German had bought it for twelve pesos and melted it down. It had been dug up in 1898 at a village called Santa Ana, a few hours' ride west of the Chihuahua boundary.

And now Ruggles was setting out once more to find Tayopa, and I was riding with him. From Chihuahua City a wooden coach, punctured by Revolutionary bullets and guarded by a squad of soldiers, took us to Miñaca, the end of rails and roads. I climbed to the summit of Cerro de la Campana, which overshadows the village, and looked at the sun as it set. Ruggles had two little tough Mexican mules under the care of a Mexican at Miñaca, and I bought two for myself. We engaged a *mozo*, who, according to the custom of the country, trotted on foot behind the pack animals. He had not been spoiled by shoes.

We meandered somewhat from the main trail, visit-

ing the falls of Baseachic, higher than Niagara's, and going by Ocampo to see a merchant who had for years been giving calico to Tarahumares in the vain hope of learning the source of certain ore they brought in for trade. We had been out nearly two weeks when we camped at La Quiparita, where we proposed to lay in a supply of meat and do some prospecting.

Apache Gold and Yaqui Silver

La Quiparita is paradise. It is in the Pima country, but no one lives there. It is marked by a group of ancient *arrastres*, wherein centuries ago Spaniards crushed ore from mines that nobody within the memory of man has known the location of. Out of the once rock-paved floors of two or three of those old *arrastres* great pines now grow. Near them is good water. For miles and miles around, the land alternates between sloping mesas and pine-clad mountains and flats. Black grama and red bunch grass grow stirrup-high; every canyon holds water — and not a hoofprint of cow or horse indents the sod. Turkeys, deer, "fool" (Mearns) quail, band-tailed pigeons, foxes, lobos and all manner of other wild life abound. Here a trail leading from the north to Morís crosses the east-and-west Sonora Trail. Haunting the cross-trails, legend says, there lived during the first twenty years of the present century a grizzly bear that preyed on travelers and was "unkillable." He had a white star in his breast, and was called "El Matador."

As we traveled and camped, the whole country was to me fresher and more enthralling than any novel of the far away and long ago I have ever read. And in this romance of the Sierra Madre, La Quiparita was the freshest chapter.

We had been here six days, awakened every morning

by the gobble of wild turkeys, and were preparing to spend our last night before moving on the next day, when our *mozo* sighted a traveler coming down the trail from the north.

He rode up to the camp. He had a good outfit, and he gave his name as Custard, though he did not look like it. He accepted the invitation to unsaddle almost before it was given. He was not a reserved man. His tongue had not had a chance at English for months. It soon came out that he was looking for Tayopa.

"I am not so much interested in the mine itself," he explained after supper, "as in the wealth supposed to be stored at Tayopa. I have a document concerning that wealth. I have a map to the location. You men are looking for the mine. I'm for pooling our knowledge and searching as partners, you to have the mine and I to have the treasure."

"We have made a contract," Ruggles, with an assenting nod from myself, agreed.

Custard reached into his pocket and pulled out a long, heavy envelope. I thought I saw his hand shaking. Meantime Ruggles threw a fresh chunk of pitch pine upon the fire — our only light. The air was chilly, but as Ruggles bent over I saw perspiration on his face. Custard held the envelope in his hand a full minute without opening it. Then he put it back into his pocket.

"Before I show the papers to you," he said, "you had better know how I came by them. They are not originals, but they are true copies. They have a history."

The history, stripped of various geographical and biographical details, was this. A number of years back General Antonio Hernandez of Nogales was buying cattle in eastern Sonora. While he was in a poverty-stricken little pueblo called Guadalupe de Santa Ana, an old Indian woman whom the general chanced to meet asked him if he would deliver a letter to the priest in Guaymas, on the Gulf of California. General Hernandez told the old woman that he expected to be in Guaymas within a month or so and that he would then deliver the letter.

"It is a very important letter," she quavered. "Father Domingo made me promise to get it delivered. He was priest of this parish. He came here in 1887 and built our church. When he died he was an old man. He was a queer man. He was always walking about and looking, looking. He was very kind to me. He left me fifty pesos and all his belongings and this letter. I have had it for two years. You are the first traveler I have seen that I could trust with it. Many thanks and may the Virgin protect you in your journey and the Saints reward you."

As General Hernandez took the long envelope he

saw that it was of inferior paper and that it was addressed and sealed. He put it in his inside coat pocket. After he left Guadalupe de Santa Ana, he spent several weeks trading for scattered bunches of cattle. When he finally reached Hermosillo, he decided not to go to Guaymas at all but to go north to Nogales, his home. He thought of the letter. He was now where the post office department functioned; he would stamp the letter and mail it.

When he removed the envelope from his pocket, he found it almost worn out and the mucilage all melted. He procured a fresh envelope and addressed it. While he was refolding the letter to place it inside the new envelope, his eye fall on the word TAYOPA.

He had heard of Tayopa all his life. It was human to examine further.

He scanned the map and read the document. Then he copied both, honorably mailing the originals to the priest at Guaymas. General Hernandez is a good businessman. It was not until he had spent more than 6000 pesos looking for Tayopa, mostly in Chihuahua, that he parted with his map and document and their history to a certain El Paso contractor with whom he had cordial business relations.

"And I," Custard concluded his explanation "am scout for that contractor."

Again he reached into his pocket, and this time he spread the papers on the ground in the full light of the fire.

The map is boldly entitled *"Mapa del Camino de Tayopa"* (Map of the Tayopa Road). It shows Tayopa to be in the Sierra Madre — certainly not a very specific location. It shows roads leading thither from two widely separated towns in western Chihuahua. It shows a great mesa called Mesa Campanero east of Tayopa and overlooking it. It represents Tayopa as being a group of "seventeen mines of good assay" in an oval valley in the center of which is the *"Yglesia"* (church). Adjacent to Tayopa, it shows the gold placers of Páramo.

The document itself is long, detailed, and formal. It consists, first, of directions for getting down to Tayopa from the Mesa Campanero; second, of directions for getting to Páramo from Tayopa; third, of a minute inventory of the riches stored and left at Tayopa by the Jesuits. It is dated February 17, 1646.

Translated, the full title of the document runs thus:

"A true and positive description of the mining camp called Real of Our Lady of Guadalupe of Tayopa, made in January, 1646, by the Right Reverend Father Guardian of Tayopa, Fray Francisco Villegas Garsona y Orosco, Royal Vicar-General of the Royal and Dis-

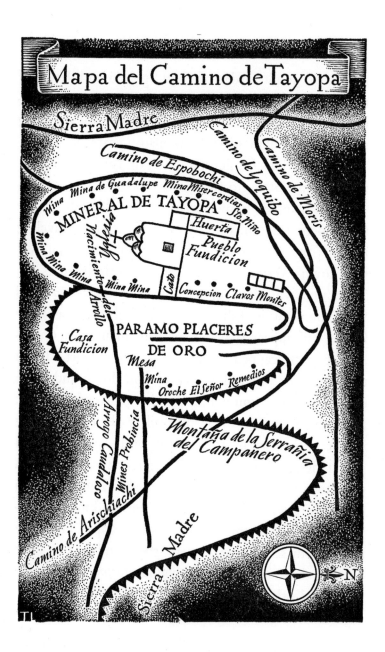

tinguished Jesuit Order of Saint Ignacio and Jesuit of
the Grand Faculty of the Province of Sonora and Bis-
calla, by the grace of God and of his Majesty the King
in Madrid, whom God keep many years."

The directions for getting down to Tayopa from the
mesa, or mountain, to the east are precise:

"First take the branch road on the left side of the
Campanero ridge in the Sierra Madre. Thus traveling
towards the west along the Arisciachi trail, you will
turn down a very narrow and broken path that cuts off.
Then you will come into a thicket of *madroño* trees
very abundant in foliage. To the right side and far
below will appear two hills or runt mountains (*cerritos chapos*) capped with red *topueste* dirt. From
the *madroños* proceed 1200 varas on down and there
on a cañon slope you will find a clump of *güérigo* trees.
Here there appears to be no trail at all, but, keeping
your course down on for a matter of 45 varas, you will
pass under two notably thick *güérigo* trees that touch
their tops with the top of a live oak. Hence the two
cerritos chapos already mentioned form a kind of gate-
way by which to enter the Real of Tayopa. The slope
between these *cerritos* is very steep and is for some
distance thick with *ocotillos*, the *torete prieto*, the *vino
ramo*, and other thorned growth.

"Descending more gradually now, you come to the

border of the valley, where are the church and the pueblo, circumscribed by seventeen mines of good assay."

The inventory of the riches declares that they are buried beneath the church. A few of the items will suggest the vast worth of the entirety.

"Item. Four bells, the largest weighing 28 *arrobas* [about seven hundred pounds] and having inscribed on it the word Tayopa, the other three being Tayopa bells also.

"Item. One bell called Remedios, weighing 11 *arrobas* and 10 pounds.

"Item. One small bell called Piedad, weighing 5 *arrobas*. All these bells were made in 1603 by Fray Lorenzo, the *campanero* [bell maker] of Tayopa.

"Item. A famous baptismal font of carved cedar inlaid with silver from the Dulces Nombres Mine.

"Item. A cut stone box filled with jewels.

"Item. A pair of processional candle holders, four golden incensories, two large golden communion plates, two silver chalices from ore from the mine called Jesús María y José, a shrine made of silver from the Santo Niño and glimmered with gold from El Páramo, and four fine stones from La Mina de los Remedios.

"Item. 65 *cargas* [pack-loads] of silver, each *carga* packed in cowhide bags and containing 8½ *arrobas*

[221]

[212 pounds] of bars from divers mines of this *Mineral*.

"Item. 11 *cargas* of gold, wrapped in cloth and cow-hide, from the placers of El Páramo.

"Item. 65 *arrobas* of Castilla ore, gold at sight, 22 carats assay, clean and without mercury, from El Páramo.

"Item. 165 *arrobas*," etc.

Two particulars in these papers seemed noteworthy. The full name of Tayopa was given as Guadalupe de Tayopa, and to get to this Guadalupe de Tayopa the Mesa Campanero was of pivotal importance. *Campanero* means *bell-maker*. If we could find the Mesa of the Bell-Maker we could get down to Tayopa — but where was that Mesa?

Now, while trying to locate the Tayopa bell found in the village of Santa Ana in 1896 and later melted down by the German in Hermosillo, Ruggles had been only two hours' ride away from the little village of Guadalupe de Santa Ana, in which place the old woman had given General Hernandez the papers belonging to the dead priest. Mexico is full of places called "Guadalupe." This Guadalupe de Santa Ana had the reputation of being a "nest of eagles," an "eagle" in this part of the Sierra Madre meaning a man tricky and murderous.

Ruggles had a theory that Sierra Obscura down the

Under the Mesa of the Bell-Maker

Río Mayo might be Mesa Campanero. "It's this way," he explained. "A mining engineer at Concheña used to have a chart. I saw it once. It called for a Mesa Campanero, a ranch named Tayopa on top of the Mesa, and an Arroyo Tayopa. The engineer made four trips to the Sierra Obscura looking for Tayopa and trying to identify the mountain as Mesa Campanero. He actually found an insignificant ranch named Tayopa — nothing else. This location seems too far south for the Tayopa mines, but a branch of the old Spanish road leads towards it, and now with this map in hand we should investigate it."

We would follow the trail, then, to Sierra Obscura, look for two runty red-capped hills under it and watch, above all, for *güérigo* trees. What kind of trees were *güérigo* trees anyhow? The *mozos* had never heard of them. Custard had a trail of his own to follow.

The Sierra Obscura is an enormous mountain that drops from pines into the hot *barrancas*. While making our way up a rough canyon on one side of it, we came to the *ranchito* called El Tigre of one Perfecto García, a pure-bred descendant of an Ópata chief, though Mexicanized in ways and speech. It was near night and the great mountain was as dark as its name. Here we camped. Perfecto had all his cattle, forty or fifty head, in a pen. He kept them there every night, he said, to protect them from the lions, bears, and jaguars. His boy, without a gun, for the ranch did not possess arms of any kind, kept four fires burning about the pen all the night long.

After ten days of fruitless explorations we camped again at Perfecto García's on our way out. The family was in great distress as well as excitement. Perfecto's brother had just come in horribly mutilated. He had been out with his dog hunting javelinas. The dog had bayed a big boar that refused to go into a cave. When the man rode up and saw the boar cutting the entrails out of the dog, he got down to attack with his machete, the only weapon he possessed. The vicious animal turned on him, and in a minute tusked his leg, his side and his face, nearly cutting off his ear. It seemed that the javelina had the man down for good, when the wounded dog rallied and made a rescue. In the end, the dog died fighting; the boar got away, doubtless to die; and the Mexican dragged in to the ranch.

Ruggles washed the wounds with carbolic soap and sewed and bandaged them up. Don Perfecto was in an expansive humor.

"Are you not hunting for mines?" he asked Ruggles.
"Yes."
"Do you have any documents to direct you?"
"Yes."

[224]

"I have one also. Let me show it to you."

Then out of the niche built into the thick stone or adobe walls of so many Mexican houses, Perfecto took a roll of *gamuza*. He unrolled this buckskin and showed a worn parchment entitled *"Conocimiento de Tayopa,"* or, as we might say, "A Chart of Identification for Tayopa." He was glad to let us copy it. Exactly translated, the opening sentences run thus:

"It is worth while to remember and never to forget that there is a famous mining camp of prodigious richness known to the *antiguos* by the name of Tayopa. Situated it is on the first flowings of the River Yaqui, on the downward slopes of the Sierra Madre, in the direction of the town of Yécora in the ancient province of Ostimuri. The smelters remain there not only with great deposits of ore of high assay but with considerable silver in bullion form, stored away just as the *antiguos* left it. During long years Ostimuri has been almost altogether depopulated." From this point in the reading the parchment was so torn and rubbed that only a few unconnected words could be made out. Perfecto García could not read the document himself, but he had had it read to him many times, he said.

"Where did you get this?" Ruggles asked.

"I will tell you," the *ranchero*, dignified by a consciousness of his lineage, replied. "It has been in my family for a very long while. As the oldest son of my father, I inherited it from him. He and some other Ópata men took it from the Pima Indians. The Pimas had driven off my people's stock. My people followed and raided a *ranchería* of the Pimas. They sacked everything the Pimas had. This *conocimiento* was in an earthen pot in a cave. With it were also some bone tools, a silver buckle, three pieces of money and a turquoise necklace. Nothing but the paper has come down. I do not know where the Pimas got it. You know all that I know."

Now the links were forging together. The district of Ostimuri at one time, I knew, comprised the southeastern part of Sonora, in which Yécora is located. Ruggles knew that directly west of Yécora lay a great mountain. Under and below this mountain lay Guadalupe de Santa Ana, where the dead priest's map to Tayopa had fallen into the hands of the cattle-buyer. If Tayopa was in Ostimuri, in the direction of Yécora, "on the first flowings of the River Yaqui, on the downward slopes of the Sierra Madre," then this big mountain west of Yécora should be the Mesa Campanero and Guadalupe de Santa Ana should be Guadalupe de Tayopa.

When we got to Yécora we created an excitement. We were the first foreigners the inhabitants had seen in two years. The Mesa Campanero? All gestures were towards the long pine-clad mountain to the west.

The trail from Yécora west skirts this mountain, looping northward so as to avoid the steep grades. On the eastern side of the Mesa the water drains into the Río Mayo; on the western side, into "the first flowings of the Río Yaqui." The crest of the broad-topped mountain is perhaps five thousand feet above the gnarled floor of the basin wherein lies Guadalupe de Santa Ana. We resolved not to "cut for sign" but to work out the ancient road according to our map.

We spent two weeks tracing this road over the Mesa and down its western slope. We found living on the Mesa two families descended from Confederate soldiers who had left the United States at the end of the Civil War swearing they would not submit to tyranny; their intermarried descendants spoke little English. Often we lost the old trace. On account of washes, we had to make wide detours. We had to work out the greater part of the route afoot. In one place we found a pavement of cobblestones. The trail came into a steep canyon called "Arroyo Hondo" and followed it downward, dropping from bench to bench. Of course it had never been used by vehicles. On some of the narrow shelves were holes that probably once supported a kind of scaffolding to widen the path.

Apache Gold and Yaqui Silver

The old *"camino real"* passed through more than one "thicket of *madroño* trees." As we proceeded on down, the long-crested and long-tailed *urracas* — Columbia jays — screamed and chattered at us like maniacs. Now and then we startled parrots.

Then we came to some immense trees, gnarled and old, the like of which none of us had seen before. They were near a seep of water, and it was well along in the afternoon when we reached them.

"We camp right here," exulted Ruggles. "I am going to find what these trees are. They were here before Columbus sailed. If they are not *güérigos*, I'll eat my hat."

He went off for the village of Santa Ana, an hour's ride distant. With him came back an old fellow named Juan, who claimed to be half-French. This Juan said that everybody in the country knew the trees as *güérigos*, and that he made chairs of the wood. I bought one of the chairs the next day, but a pack mule broke it. I have since identified the tree as *Populus wislizeni;* it is rare, and old Juan said that in his region it grew only along two canyons coming down from the Mesa Campanero.

The route as we followed it down next morning ran between two "runt hills capped with red *topueste* dirt." It led into a kind of basin of rocky hills so rough and

[228]

barren of soil that only thorns grow on them — just such a parched, bleak, barren, rocky, God-forsaken waste as marks the locality of many good mines.

Our map — the map that General Hernandez got from the old woman in Guadalupe — was indisputably made from the lay of the land. What would Guadalupe itself reveal?

As we rode into the irregular string of adobe houses built along the arroyo, we were conscious of a distinct hostility. This was the "nest of eagles." Inquiry brought us to the house of the *comisario*, the chief of the pueblo, Joaquín Flores.

He came out and greeted his visitors with three very blunt questions: "Where are you from? Where are you going? What do you want?"

If all the questions, especially the third one, were answered directly and truthfully, the reception would probably be still less cordial. Ruggles was parrying words when the wife of the *comisario* came out wringing her hands and crying, "Succor in the name of the Little Mother of the Holy Child!"

"What is the matter?" Ruggles asked. We were still on our horses, as we had not been asked to dismount.

"Our son is dying with the fever of influenza," Joaquín Flores stoically replied. "Our whole village is cursed with the disease."

"Have you a doctor?"

Ruggles well knew that the question was superfluous. Then he added, "Let me see your son."

He was led inside. Presently he came out, unpacked the mule that carried his medicines, and selected a bottle of fever drops. The effect of the drug and of cold water that the parents were prevailed upon to allow the patient was immediate.

Joaquín became an entirely different man.

"Unload your saddles and your packs under my roof," he said. "I have corn in abundance and wood. Here is your house. I am at your orders. All I have is yours."

He commanded a feast. He gave a dance in our honor that very night. The next day he placed a cabin at our disposal. He would not think of letting us go until our beasts had recruited and he had guided us to a choice game region near his ranch out in the mountains.

IV · "Tayopa is Here"

Within three days' time Ruggles had doctored fifty people, some of them brought in from as far as twenty miles away. For instance, a girl was brought in with face so swollen from poison ivy that she could open neither eyes nor mouth. With solutions of soda and potassium permanganate Ruggles cured her. Her father and brother offered themselves "as slaves" in payment. They had nothing with which to pay, they said. Ruggles never took pay for his medical services.

In such an atmosphere of gratitude and trust it was easy to broach the vital subject — mines — and, when the siege of patients relented somewhat, to prospect openly. Every native of the village could show evidences of ancient workings and tell their names: El Refugio, El Santo Niño, El Apache, La Barbayeña, La Bronzuda, Los Dulces Nombres, the whole circle of seventeen mines — "of good assay," we hoped. We found the ruins of *vasos* (smelters). We found five enormous slag piles, into which natives yet "gopher" for slugs of silver — for the old system of smelting was notoriously wasteful. We picked up pieces of tools, locks, and other objects evidently of Spanish usage.

Meantime the Guadalupe men were unlocking their

"word hoards" to add to the evidence. If there is any one thing that the men of Guadalupe excel in, it is in telling tales. In the summertime they shift their positions with the crawling shade and talk. In the wintertime they squat in the sunshine and talk. The nights were made for talking, they say. Their women, like the women of their Indian ancestors, do all the work.

Flipper had been inclined to discount the tradition of a great treasure "secured in a tunnel or prison vault, the entrance to which was barred by an iron door 2281 varas east and 63 varas south of the church door." Not so that excellent man and true friend, Don Joaquín Flores, though he knew nothing of such exact measurements. I try to repeat his tale as he told it in a low voice behind the curiously carved doors of his house.

"I am getting to be an old man," he began. "I have lived here all my life. In my time I have seen many searchers for mines and lost treasures come into these mountains. Some of them never went out. Listen.

"When I was nine years old, my mother and my aunt set out one afternoon to look for the milk cows on that little red mountain of *topueste* dirt east of the church. I remember that my aunt did not want to go. She was fat and liked to stay by the fire and toast *tortillas*. While they were gone, a very hard rain came. They

[232]

got under a cliff. It rained and it rained. Water was running in all the gullies; everything was wet. They could no longer look for the cows. So when the rain let up, they started home.

"They decided to bring some wood with them, and in order to get it dry they pulled dead sticks off the bushes as they passed. As they were coming down the hill with an armful each, they all of a sudden came to where the earth had parted — parted wide open. There was a great crack wider across than a horse could jump. No crack had ever been at that place before.

"They put their wood down and knelt over to observe. They saw — I will swear to you that this is true — an iron door. They could reach the top of it, but they could not budge it or see what was behind it. They wanted to open it. Then they came home in a great hurry and secretly told my father what they had seen. He was ready to return to the iron door at once, but another great rain began to fall, a cloudburst. Then came the darkness.

"The next morning very early my mother and my aunt and my father went to look for the iron door. But there was no crack left in the earth. The crack had closed up, leaving not even a scar. Of course the water

[233]

had washed out all tracks, but it was easy to trail the
two women by the bushes off which they had broken
pieces of dry sticks. On the very spot where they had
put down their loads while they peeped at the iron
door, were bits of wood. There was no chance of missing the route they had traveled.

"The whole village soon learned the story and everybody turned out to hunt the iron door. It was of no use. Then the people began to make fun of my mother and my aunt. I cannot tell you how much shame these two had. They had told something that appeared to be false. Years afterwards I saw them more than once kneel before the Virgin of Guadalupe in our church and pray that somehow their words about the iron door might be proved true.

"As for me, I know the words were true. Some say there is a great treasure in the tunnel. Some say the treasure is under the church. I do not know where it is."

At this point it is necessary to say that the Guadalupeñas are divided in opinion as to where the original church of the village stood. Some claim that the present church, built by Father Domingo in 1888, stands exactly on the spot occupied by the first mission church, which was destroyed so far back that no one knows when. Others claim that the original site was up the hill; still others that it was down the hill. The "Italian writer" had no doubts on the matter. His story is common property.

This odd character came to Guadalupe about 1910. He claimed to be a historian interested in writing a true record of the Indians and their relations with the Spaniards. Somehow he won the confidence of the natives and secured their permission to build a one-roomed adobe cabin fifty feet north of the church. The foundation of the cabin still shows.

These huts, of course, have only dirt floors. The Italian got a table made of *güérigo* wood. Then he claimed that his writing table would not stand level on the dirt floor. So he had a platform of wood made about six feet square on which to set it. The platform was placed in the back end of his room.

The "writer" explained that he was very sensitive to noises and could write only at night, when all was silent. He slept by day. Seldom was he seen. After he had been quietly sleeping by day and presumably writing by night for about two months, a citizen very late one night passed between the historian's cabin and the church. He heard, he thought, sounds coming from the earth beneath his feet. He paused, put his ear down. He heard distinctly the slow, muffled, regular sound of a pick digging into the earth far below. He thought that perhaps some Indian ancestor of his, doomed in death as in life to labor in the tunnel of a mine, was picking down there. He had heard ghostly workmen before, heard them breathing hard, grunting, calling for food and drink. He felt sorry for this *pobrecito*. He was disturbed too. Somehow the picking seemed to differ from the picking of the spirits with which he was so familiar. He decided to rouse the *comisario* and tell him what was going on.

The mayor was a man of decision and a hard head. He ordered six able-bodied men up, and they all went to investigate the strange sounds coming out of the ground near their church. They were silent, and they kept in the shadows. They saw a little slit of light coming through the closed door of the historian's house. According to the common architectural style of the country, it had no window.

Presently the door opened and a man stepped outside with what appeared to be a loaded bucket in each hand. He felt the way with his feet for a few seconds until his eyes grew accustomed to the darkness; then he walked rapidly down to the creek, which is about fifty steps below the church. It is usually dry, but at this time was running. The man emptied his buckets into the water. While he was away, the sound of the picking was not heard. Shortly after he re-entered the cabin, the picking began again. Then again there was quietness and the man emerged with two more loaded buckets. He was making for the creek when the citizens seized him. The buckets contained earth.

Examination of the cabin showed that the wooden platform was being used to conceal the entrance to a small shaft. Twelve feet down it became a tunnel two feet wide and three feet deep. It was barely large enough to admit of a man's working in it, but it had penetrated to within eighteen feet of the foundation of the church.

The next morning the mayor called the men of the village together, got a handful of small sticks of uneven length, and directed each man to draw one. The four men drawing the four shortest sticks were delegated to "escort" the Italian historian forth.

"And you know," concluded one of the "eagles" who told the story, "we never found a scrap of paper on his body."

The cabin was razed to the ground. A year later two well-equipped Italians came to Guadalupe to make inquiry concerning their compatriot. "He has left the country," was the only answer they received. They found it fitting to leave the country also.

One night after we had been in Guadalupe de Santa Ana long enough to know most of the men by name, I stepped up to the hut of old Apolonio Daniel.

"*Oiga!* Listen!" he began as soon as I was securely inside. "One time I opened up a vein in that ancient Refugio Mine and took out eleven *quinientos* pounds [a *quiniento* is five hundred] of ore. It was good ore, but I had reason not to continue working it. Someone else that I could not see was working also in that

[238]

mine. I kept hearing the sounds of hammer and pick
other than my own. I thought at first that the sounds
might be echoes of my work. So I stopped. But the
other sounds kept on. The poor fellow making them
was away down there in the ground. He could stop

[239]

only for a few minutes in the middle of the day. He seemed to get no rest at all. Sometimes I could hear him crying out, '*Tor-ti-ll-as, tor-ti-ll-as, tor-ti-ll-as*,' as if he were hungry as well as tired. Then he would beg for water, '*Agua, agua, agua*.' Often I could hear him gasp out with each blow of his heavy pick, '*Ah-uhh, ah-uhh, ah-uhh*.' There are strange things in these tunnels of the ancients."

And the Guadalupe folk had not only a great many tales about mines and treasures pertaining to their village, but also written directions for finding Tayopa. The rich man of the town, who was mayor when the Italian writer came, gave one *derrotero* (chart). Drunken old Enrique Daniel sold the second for ten pesos. Francisco Beltrán, the village saddler and chair-maker, bestowed the third. All the *derroteros* were heir-looms, and all of them corroborated the documents that Ruggles already possessed.

Francisco Beltrán had a story to go with his. About 1858, as he told, his father, who was a chemist (or assayer) and also a saddler, set out from the state of Querétaro, Mexico, with nineteen other men, to look for Tayopa. The party was in charge of a Jesuit. It consisted of two assayers, a surveyor, two assistant surveyors, three blacksmiths, one tanner, five smelter men, one treasurer, and five packers.

"Tayopa is Here"

They wandered about in the Sierra Madre for two years, several of the number dropping by the wayside. Then in a fight with some Indians all but eight were killed. They finally reached Tayopa — "this place," as Francisco emphasized. Their actions aroused suspicions and an attack. Only Beltrán escaped. He got into a cave, where during a long period of concealment an Indian girl supplied him with food and water. In the end he married the Indian girl and came to Guadalupe to live. After Francisco, their tenth child, was born in 1874, the father wrote out from memory the *derrotero* that the Jesuit directing the searching party had shown him. Thus it has been preserved.

Every inhabitant of Guadalupe seemed to know what we had been trying to find out. Some of the men and most of the women had never been twenty miles from their birthplace; and there were no immigrants among them. Why, always belly-pinched and never without time to spare, had not some of the holders of the secret unearthed at least a modicum of the rich ore at their elbows or a handful of the millions stored at their feet? Ask why for generations the women have carried water on their heads, during all but the rainy season, from a hole a mile up the creek, when a few hours of work in the sand and gravel of the creek would afford a well of water immediately at hand. There is

[241]

always a full answer to such questions: "God did not will it."

We notified Custard that we had found Tayopa. Ruggles and I were still trying to obtain fair samples of ore from the old tunnels, most of them caved in, when he arrived. Of course he would as a matter of prudence have to secure an official concession before bringing into the sunlight such a vast treasure as his waybill called for. We told Custard of a recent episode in Tayopa history.

A few months before our arrival, as was narrated to us with iterated detail, a "rich Arabe" — and an "Arabe" may be a Jew, an Assyrian, or of some other nationality — arrived from the west with a concession signed by General Plutarco Elías Calles, then president of the Republic of Mexico, a guard of forty soldiers, and several laborers. His concession, which he showed with ostentation, called upon the authorities of Guadalupe de Santa Ana to allow him to excavate under the church or anywhere around it. The mayor and all the citizens were angry at such desecration, but with the military order and the forty soldiers in front of them they could do nothing but yield. Not a hand of the village, though, could the "Arabe" hire to dig.

His men dug holes through the church floor and brought up skeletons — "nothing more." The people sat around on the ridges watching. The diggers struck a rock shelf underlying the church, but this they did not penetrate. Around the church they put down holes that we saw, yet unfilled. Then they left.

The matter was too good a theme for a native ballad-maker to miss. He made up a long string of verses commenting on the attempts of the "Arabe." Don Apolonio's five daughters, ranging from the motherly eldest, twelve years old, down to the snaggle-toothed baby, sang it with much more charm than the verses contained in themselves. In the translation of the three verses that follow, the original rhythm is not much injured: —

If they wish to take the riches
They'll break their heads.
The church three hundred years old
Is situated on a mesa —
Which is not far from here.

Let them go up on top of the mesa,
Should the Arabe prolong his stay.
There above is another church
And a well full of silver —
Which is not far from here.

Now with this I say farewell.
We are speaking of things in the past.
Here ends the ballad.
Meanwhile we know enough to quit —
For we do not live far from here.

Apache Gold and Yaqui Silver

Custard was sure that the treasure must be under the rock that the "Arabe's" forces did not penetrate; yet he had the fate of the "Italian historian" and the outspoken attitude towards the "Arabe" to consider. Getting to that treasure was a business that would have to wait, be prepared for by something more than an official concession. So far as I know, the business is still waiting.

To clean out and explore the old tunnels and to forward any real work would require capital. We estimated that merely to denounce — survey and lay legal claim to — the far-spread *pertenencias* of land enclosing the scattered workings would take a year and more money than either of us had. After all, we had found no paying ore. My own small interest I turned over to Ruggles, fully realizing that I was still in debt to him. From a company of lawyers and engineers in El Paso, he raised enough capital to make denouncements and do some assay work. But the rich vein has not yet been struck.

V · "Can You Read Shadder Writing?"

Nothing is ever settled until it is settled right — and nothing is ever settled right until it is settled in *my way*. Facts are stubborn things, but theories are stubborner. When a man becomes thoroughly convinced that a lost mine is in a certain area, nothing can unfix the idea. If the mine were found by somebody else in another area, he would merely say that it must be another mine and not *the* lost mine he was looking for at all. People are going to go on looking for Tayopa in many places.

One time I was riding in the Sierra Madre a long, long way from where Ruggles and I located Tayopa. I was riding for something better than gold or silver; I was riding for the elation of being free and having plenty of room. One evening — or late *afternoon,* as some people call it — we came to good water and I told my *mozo* we'd make camp. Before long three Mexicans rode up and camped not far off. I was glad to have their company, for I knew I'd learn something about the country and its traditions from them. Soon we were all cooking at the same fire. They had some fresh roasting ears that, roasted in the shuck in hot ashes, were the juiciest and most toothsome corn I have ever tasted.

These Mexicans were of the peasant but not peon class, just and kind-hearted and gracious. I noticed a blowing horn that one of them had. It was very long, and on it was carved in bold, rude lettering, VIVA DIOS (LONG LIVE GOD). The sun was going down through a gap in the mountains, and just as a great boulder beside the trail crossing fell into shadow, the owner of the horn mounted the boulder and began to blow. His blasts made, it seemed to me, the trees tremble, and echoes answered back from far away.

"Can you hear it?" the blower asked of his companions.

"No," one answered.

"Not yet," replied the other.

The man went on blowing and blasting. I shifted my position for the comfort of my ears. The horn-blower's two companions were shifting around, cupping their ears, bending this way and that way, standing silent with open hands raised near their ears, seemingly searching for some sound as delicate as the last, low, solitary chirp of a cricket in late fall. The blowing and listening went on until dark. The men, who said nothing, were quite serious, though now and then they smiled at some attempted levity on my part. Eventu-

ally this levity gave way to a consuming curiosity. I waited until after supper to ask questions.

"We are trying to find the echo of Tayopa," the horn-blower said. "Tayopa is in a canyon maybe not far from this place. The conductor of the mule train that carried the silver out from Tayopa was a forefather of mine long passed away. When he reached this crossing, he always blew his horn to announce his arrival. The sound would echo; then that echo would echo. The place where this third echo was made was Tayopa — perhaps a certain crevice in the rock, perhaps a tunnel mouth — who knows? The third echo would not come as such, but sounded as clear as the original blast, only shriller. This is a tradition with us. We know we are near Tayopa, but we cannot find it, and we are hoping this horn will tell us."

The next morning I left rather early. As I mounted my mule, the good man mounted the boulder again, a smile on his face and Viva Dios in his hand. I heard its blasts a good while after a turn in the trail shut out all view.

Not long ago, standing in the lobby of a Western hotel, I heard my name called. A stranger introduced himself. He had heard that I was interested in Tayopa.

"Can you read shadder writing?" he asked abruptly.

"Not very well," I replied. We sat down off to one

side. He pulled a paper out of his pocket and unfolded it. It contained a diagram of five rocks and a reproduction of certain symbols found on each of the rocks.

"You can't see the figures on these rocks," he said, "until they are in shadder, at a certain time of day." The man told me he had made eleven trips hunting for Tayopa, that on a certain mesa west of the Mayo River he had discovered the rocks and the "shadow writing" on them. The trouble was that, though he knew the writing pointed the way to Tayopa, he couldn't read it.

There is nothing shadowy about John Williams, range foreman of William Randolph Hearst's great hacienda, La Babícora, in western Chihuahua. I must try to paint his picture before I tell the story he told me. All of his sixty years have been spent in the mountains of New Mexico, Arizona and Old Mexico — mostly in the Sierra Madre. He was on the Babícora when it was unfenced and maverick bulls and cows of the long-horn breed would run for thirty miles, once they got a good scare from mounted men. His father was a Mormon bishop, "not very orthodox," and the cast of his own faith makes him what's called a "jack Mormon." He reads books. The Mexicans call him Don Juan, and so does everybody else. He has a cheerful, easy way, is always smoking a pipe, unless he is chewing native tobacco. He is a "star boarder," and a Mexican cook can't get the meat or beans too hot with chili for him. Maybe that's why he still does not have to let out the wreathing strap in order to girt himself up. He's come to think tequila just about as good as whisky, but does not take too much of either. He breaks in his Stetson hats so that the knot in the band, supposed to be worn on the left side of the head, is in front. He loves to talk, and his hesitating drawl, as easy as breathing, should be recorded to illustrate for the next generation how natural the human voice could be before the automatons who jabber incessantly over radios ruined it.

"A mighty long time ago," Don Juan said, while we sat one winter night by a fire in the big ranch house at La Babícora, Mr. William Randolph Hearst not being aware of our existence and we not being concerned about his — "A mighty long time ago I was riding early one morning in the Sierra Madre away west of the town now called Madera. A cousin was with me. We were heading around a prong of the Rio Bonito and got to a point where we could look down into the barranca. It looked as deep as the Grand Canyon. Then across from us, on the other side, but up a long ways from the bottom, I caught a glimpse of some cliff-houses. There are lots of 'em in the canyons of this country, deserted a thousand years ago, they say, and nowadays these here archæologists are discovering them. They haven't discovered some way-back ones yet, however.

"I never was much of a hand to walk, but I'd walk anywhere to be where a white man has never been. It was just an accident that I caught sight of those cliff-houses. The canyon walls camouflage 'em like a clump of sagebrush does a jack rabbit squatted down. Nobody lived in that country, and nobody lives in it yet. Nobody's lived there, I guess, since the cliff people disappeared. Here was one place, I thought, where a white man had never stepped. We got down off our horses about eight o'clock in the morning. It was four that afternoon when we crawled back in the saddles. They felt better'n any rocking chair, I can tell you. In those eight hours we hadn't done anything but climb down and climb up.

"The cliff-houses were undisturbed all right. Cord ropes made out of sotol fiber still hung from some of the rafters. We saw grains of corn on little red cobs in fiber baskets. There were all sorts of *metates* and grinding stones. Things hadn't been disturbed at all. But another white man had been there ahead of us. His name was on a wall, scrawled with charcoal — Joe B. Taylor, 1877 — the year I was born. What Joe B. Taylor was doing down there in 1877 or who Joe Taylor was, I had no more idea than the man in the moon.

"Well, about twenty years later — it was in 1914, I recollect — a young feller named Taylor dragged into Chuichupa and found Dave Brown. A man with one of those sixty-foot California riatas could jest about rope all there is of Chuichupa and drag it down the canyon. Dave Brown is a Mormon rancher, and's had more experience than anybody else with those renegade Apaches that still live like wild animals in the country west of him.

"This young feller Taylor told Dave Brown he'd left his outfit of mules in a boxed-up neck of the Rio Arros three or four days' foot-travel back. Left 'em in a place he'd got 'em into and couldn't get 'em out of. The Rio Bonito, on a prong of which I'd seen those cliff-houses with Joe B. Taylor's name written on a wall, flows into the Rio Arros. I guess that country in there is jest about God's masterpiece, as far as roughness goes.

"This young feller Taylor went on to tell how away back in the Seventies his pa, Joe B. Taylor, took tuberculosis and had to go west to live. He drifted into prospecting, found enough for a little stake, and then got off down into Mexico. He thought he'd find the Lost Tayopa Mine maybe, and had it figgered out as being in the Rio Arros country. He worked up the

Arros until he come to where the Rio Bonito cut in, and then he took up the Bonito. He was making a good sketch map of the canyons all the time he was prospecting. Seems he'd had some training in a school at that sort of thing. He didn't know the names of any of the side canyons, but he could sure draw. I saw the map. He had those cliff-houses marked on the map, and it wasn't far from them he struck gold. He didn't claim it to be Tayopa gold, but still he thought Tayopa must be somewhere in reach of it. It was placer gold he found.

"He took some of it down to Temosachic to trade off for provisions. That took him five days' traveling maybe, but when he got there he was afraid if he showed the gold somebody would shadow him and trail him back to his placer. He went on down to Guerrero, three days' more travel, to trade in his gold and get supplies. Then he corkscrewed around in all sorts of ways so's to throw anybody off the direction he'd come from. Finally he got back to the gold. He took out seventy-five thousand dollars' worth, and then pulled for the States. He died in San Francisco, leaving the map and all to his boy. I'm jes' telling what this boy told Dave Brown.

"The boy growed up some, and he was trying to find his pa's placer gold and maybe Tayopa too when he got his mules boxed up in the Rio Arros. He'd had a plenty of the country. He offered Dave Brown the mules and the map if Dave would get him to the railroad at Casas Grandes and buy him a ticket to El Paso. Dave traded with him and was actually able to locate the mules and get 'em out. He and I took that map and tried to find the placer. There was too much walking involved to suit either one of us, I guess."

The chances for long, long searches for Tayopa are still good. I will tell you why.

One raw, cold, windy day many years ago, Gus McGinnis — another boss on the Babícora ranch now — was working on a windmill in the Casas Grandes country. Finally, almost too stiff with cold to climb down the ladder, he descended to warm himself at a fire.

"I have a good mind to quit windmilling and go find Tayopa," he idly remarked to the air around him.

"If you wish to know where Tayopa is," a Mexican helper rejoined, "ask Don Rafael."

"Don" by courtesy, the aged Rafael was a kind of pensioner on the ranch. He lived in a *jacal* only a short distance away, and about dinnertime he came down to the windmillers' camp.

"Say, Don Rafael," McGinnis joked him, "I hear you know where Tayopa is."

"That is true."

"Then why don't you go and get some of the wealth and relieve your family from such poverty?"

"It is a matter of honor," old Rafael solemnly answered. Then he explained.

A long, long time back, while he was a little boy, he used to go with his father to carry freight, by pack mules, into Sonora. One camp they always made was at a prosperous hacienda about a day's ride south of Dolores, in Sonora. Headquarters on this hacienda was a considerable village. The owner was not an ambitious or proud man, however. He was always friendly. He seemed to think a great deal of Rafael's father, and he was always very kind to the boy. His name was Don Miguel.

Well, one time while the freighter and his son were about to load their mules in Temosachic, where the stage line to Chihuahua City terminated, they met two Spaniards outfitting to go into the mountains to look for Tayopa. It happened that the same stage which brought in the Spaniards brought also a message for Rafael's father to proceed to Chihuahua City. He had confidence in his son, however, and he told him to lose no time in getting the mules packed and starting on the long trip into Sonora. They had a faithful hired man who was as good a packer and freighter as the father.

Everything went well on the trip. As usual Rafael made camp at the prosperous hacienda a day's ride south of Dolores. That night the owner, Don Miguel, came out to the campfire, where Rafael sat alone, the hired man having gone to visit one of his *amigos* in the village. Don Miguel always asked his friends traveling west the news from Chihuahua and about certain people living along the route. He himself traveled it once every year.

The chief news Rafael had to tell this time was about his father's journey to Chihuahua City and about the Tayopa seekers outfitting in Temosachic.

"Well, they will never find Tayopa," Don Miguel said.

He and the boy were then silent for a long time. Then the good old owner of the hacienda spoke again.

"I think a great deal of your father," he said to Rafael. "He is a most honest man and is to be trusted always. You are going to be like him, I think. May God so will! I am going to tell you something that may be of value to you and save you much trouble and prevent you from wasting your time as so many men waste it — hunting Tayopa."

"Thank you," Rafael said.

"Listen!" Don Miguel went on. "My forefathers were peons in the Tayopa mines. The tradition which says Indians broke out and killed the people and covered up the mine workings is true. But the father of many of my forefathers escaped. That was long, long, long anterior to our times. This forefather was Indian, pure blood. He went away from Tayopa and was gone many years. Then he returned. He lived on at Tayopa until he died. His descendants, generation after generation, kept on living at Tayopa. They still live at Tayopa. Listen! Tayopa is here. This hacienda is Tayopa."

The old owner of the hacienda stood up before the boy there by the dim campfire and swept his arm around him. His voice was quiet.

"See that chapel?" he pointed to the old church of the hacienda. "True it has been rebuilt, but that is the chapel of Tayopa, the original. Under it is the treasure of Tayopa. You see us prosperous here. The revolutions have hardly touched us away out in these sierras. The father of my forefathers laid a command upon his line that they must never be greedy for the money, but said they might use it when in need. So, when we need money, we go a secret way to the vault and get it.

"I have told you this to save you trouble. I have given your honor something to keep."

Don Rafael, the pensioned peon, gave his account with much earnestness, with many gestures, leading by dim motions and falling voice into the centuries that are gone. In conclusion he anticipated a reflection that might be placed upon his honor for having revealed the secret.

"Now you understand," he said, "why it is I do not go and possess any of the Tayopa money. Also you will understand why I do not tell you the name of the

"Can You Read Shadder Writing?"

hacienda south of Dolores. And listen! My directions are not precise. And Don Miguel — may his soul rest in peace with the Mother of Jesus! — had another name. Yet I have told the truth."

Scalp Hunters' Ledge

SCALP HUNTERS' LEDGE

While strong-man Atlas held up the earth he stood on a turtle. The turtle this very earthy story stands on is — or was — John C. Beasley. He himself had to stand on something. That something was, under one foot, the silver ledge, and under the other the scalp hunters of the Sierra Madre.

Not since Atlas held this earth up has there been on it a wilder, a harder, a more enormous land than the Sierra Madre of the North during the days of the *Indios broncos* and the hunters of their scalps. The Yaquis, who almost never ranged outside their own territory, held the western slopes. The Apaches roamed the roughest fastnesses along the Continental Divide. The Comanches, joined by more Apaches, raided through the eastern spurs and across the plateaus clear into Durango and Zacatecas. The only reason the raiders allowed any Mexican ranchers and settlements to exist at all, they said, was to raise horses and meat for them. As regular as the "Mexican moon" of September waxed and waned, cooling the desert and filling the rock water-holes with water, the Comanches swept down, killing whatever men dared resist, capturing girls and boys to develop into squaws and warriors, and rounding up vast herds of horses to drive back north, sometimes a

[263]

thousand miles to their camps of tepees covered with painted buffalo hides on the banks of the Arkansas River. For the Comanches the wealth of nations consisted of horses, and, not because of its silver and gold but because of its horses, Mexico was for them the "treasure house of the world." Across the Staked Plains and through that wide waste south of the Rio Bravo del Norte called the Bolsón de Mapimí, the Comanche Trail stretched away, a wavering line of many trails diverging and converging, as plain as the deep-beaten scars marking the Oregon Trail or the Overland Trail when a nation migrated west in wagons.

In those times London was not nearly so far separated from Boston by the Atlantic Ocean as the Central Government in Mexico City was separated by canyons, mountains and arid mesas from its frontier states. The Central Government did nothing against the savage raiders of the north. The state governments of Chihuahua, Sonora and Durango and the meagerly armed citizens of those territories were impotent to act for themselves. Then arose a class of men without parallel in North American history — the scalp hunters. The north country was rich in silver. It was minted by the long ton; cordons of mules carried it in bars to Vera Cruz and other ports; wagons freighted it in coined pesos from Chihuahua City to Saint Louis and Indianola on the Texas coast. The state governments decided to offer silver to foreign adventurers to do what their own citizens could not do — put down the raiders.

The bounties fixed on scalps varied, a male Apache or Comanche scalp bringing at one time two hundred pesos, a female scalp or a female prisoner, one hundred and fifty pesos, and a child — to be peoned, enslaved — one hundred pesos. Generally the bounty was lower, a prime scalp at one time being valued only at a good Mexican pony. The bounties were not always fairly paid. The offers began along in the 1830's and continued intermittently into the Seventies. Chihuahua was the principal hunting ground, but, in addition to Sonora and Durango, Coahuila at one time paid bounties, and in the Forties the Governor's Palace at Santa Fe was ornamented with festoons of dried Indian ears brought in by hirelings.

The most famous of the scalp hunters was James Kirker, written down in Spanish records as Santiago Querque. He was an Irishman. He had lived with the wild Indians before he made a contract to scalp them. His dress and horse trappings combined the richness of a Spanish hidalgo with the bizarre of a Comanche chief. In a land where all men rode daringly, he was distinguished as a daring rider. With his horse going at full speed, he would lean over so that his long hair swept the ground, and, like the Comanches, he could hold a mounted position with one heel, at the same time shooting from under his horse's neck.

Next to Kirker in reputation was John Glanton. He had taken training in Texas under Mustang Gray, the most daring and relentless killer of Mexicans the border has ever known. While serving as a Texas ranger in the Mexican War, Glanton killed a Mexican civilian, "out of line of duty," for not appearing to know that *halt* — spoken in Spanish — meant *stop*. When General Taylor issued an order to put the ranger in irons, his Texas commander faced old Rough and Ready in defiance and immediately thereafter advised Glanton to "light a shuck." He seems to have lit it for Chihuahua. Hunting scalps, with him, were the Brown brothers, and after the band found that substituting Mexican hair for Apache would not longer draw a bounty, Charlie Brown established the famous Congress Hall at Tucson. The floor was paved with a mixture of desert sand, bull's blood, and cactus juice.

Then there was the Prussian Jew Speyer, who as a leading trader down the trail from Santa Fe was more an aid to the bounty hunters than one of them. Not so the Englishman Johnson. On one occasion he invited a horde of Apaches to a feast and then, while they were gorging, fired into them with a cannon he had concealed under some saddles and flour sacks. Over in Durango the most active scalper was Edward A. Weyman, who had been an officer in the privateering navy of the Republic of Texas and then the first sheriff on the Rio Grande border.

What a precious crew these scalp hunters made! They saw the elephant and heard the owl in places that no other white man knew existed. About 1860 one of them named Jim Box came back to Texas, whence he had gone fifteen years before, to tell of gold fields enormously rich discovered through Indians in Durango. He raised an expedition of around three hundred souls, including women and children, to go and possess the gold. Many died on the way, but he rode into the city of Durango with fifty fine men all mounted on white horses — a "sign of their pacific intentions." The gold must have been a myth.

The silver ledge wasn't. When the gold rush for California began in 1849, men not only crossed the Rocky Mountains through various passes, sailed around the Horn, and went over the Isthmus of Panama, but some of the more daring undertook the route from the mouth of the Rio Grande to Chihuahua City and thence over the Sierra Madre to some port on the Pacific Coast, there to ship for San Francisco. Thus, even while traveling, they could prospect in a country known to be

highly mineralized. The men who rode this way were mostly frontiersmen. At least one party of them tarried in Chihuahua to hunt Apaches and collect a little expense money on scalps.

And this brings us to John C. Beasley's story. I am as sure that he saw the ledge of silver as I am that for thirty-odd years I knew him as a truth-teller without the least propensity for inventing situations, a deer hunter familiar with an enormous country, a lawyer of the old school used to reviewing human evidence, and a man of property utterly without illusions. He was by no means the first man to see the silver, though probably the last. I see him now as in his law office he told what I have set down. I see his eyes gleaming through the moisture of years that have for him since ended forever. I hear his voice going into indistinct gutturals.

"It was in the fall of 1879 when news of a big strike of silver at Sierra Mojada in western Coahuila came across the border. Sierra Mojada was heralded as a second Comstock. I was young then, had a little money, and was full of vinegar. My dear friend Will Smith and I threw in together, outfitted with a spring wagon and four little dun Spanish mules, and pulled our freight for the diggings. We crossed the Rio Grande at Eagle Pass.

Apache Gold and Yaqui Silver

"When we got down to the Sierra Mojada, we found the country swarming with men and not nearly enough silver to go round. In fact, the mines petered out before long. While we were milling around, we ran into several other Texans from our part of the country. Among them were Captain Burris and a man with a club foot named Heath. We camped with them. They'd been pardners in California during the boom days, and this second attack of mining fever seemed worse on them than the first. They were going on farther, they declared, into New Mexico or Arizona or maybe Chihuahua, and keep going until they made a strike.

"One of several leads they talked about was a silver ledge down in western Chihuahua. They'd been carrying that lead in mind since California days, back thirty years, when they'd fallen in with three other Texans — tough hombres, I gathered, but I can't remember their names — who had done a little scalp hunting in Chihuahua before crossing the Sierra Madre for the gold fields. While trailing Apaches northwest of Chihuahua City, a considerable party of these scalp hunters had run into a ledge of silver, a kind of outcrop, enormously rich. They roached a few Apaches close to a spring not far from the silver, collected the bounty, and then headed across for California. At that time they were not looking for silver. They were bound for gold, and

nothing but gold would satisfy them. When they got
to the land of gold they split up, but three of them
hung together. These three, when Heath and Burris
met them, were down on their luck and were talking
about raising an expedition to go back and mine the
silver. They had samples to back up their account. It
would have taken a strong force to open up a mine
in the middle of Apache territory in Chihuahua. When
I went in there thirty years later it was bronco a-plenty.
Like everybody else in California at the time, Heath
and Burris were hell-bent on gold. They didn't get any
kind of way-bill to the silver ledge — just the story and
a vague idea of its geographical location. Now they
were recalling what details they could.

"When they pulled out from the Sierra Mojada, they
didn't know where they were going, except on west.
They took the road back to Eagle Pass, from which
place they planned to ride on north until they struck
the stage route between San Antonio and El Paso. They
had a strong wagon, a pair of Missouri mules sixteen
hands high, and plenty of camp equipment and shooting implements. Captain Burris, as I happened to learn,
had a money belt stuffed full of gold eagles.

"After they pulled out, Will Smith and I pirooted
round Sierra Mojada three or four days longer. Then
we decided we hadn't had enough of the mining fever

either and concluded to keep going also. When we got to Eagle Pass, we learned how our old friends had tarried there and picked up two other men. One of them was described as being youngish with an indoors look; the other, as a fine-looking, large-framed, well-preserved man of perhaps seventy years.

"Will Smith and I set out on their trail, those four little Spanish mules we drove to the spring wagon trotting right along. Then in that high, wild country between Devil's River and the Pecos we overtook the big wagon. The men in it were not a bit glad to see us. In fact, they appeared sullen and resentful of our company. We were not intending to dog them, but now that we had come together we could hardly separate without an open rupture. The country was virtually uninhabited, and west of the Pecos we stood a good chance of running into Apaches. Gradually the crowd thawed out, and old man Heath grew exceedingly cordial. He had a reason, for he was cook of the outfit, and getting around on his club foot was not easy. Will Smith and I proved right handy in carrying water, dragging up wood, and otherwise helping around camp. I was then, as I have always been, an eager hunter, and I kept the outfit supplied with fresh venison.

"One night after a bait of especially fat venison and cornbread made with grease from a young bear I had rolled over, Heath and Burris told us the story of the two strangers traveling with them. They swore that nothing less than fate had brought them together. The younger of the two strangers, McNeill by name, was from Saint Louis, where he had been clerking in a hotel. He added freely to the narrative. I was to learn later that he would do to ride any river with. The elder man was from San Francisco and other points west. His name was Fancher.

"Well, Fancher and McNeill were bound for that ledge of silver discovered by the scalp hunters. Fancher was the commanding-general, and he was taking Heath and Burris in with him. Like them, he had been a forty-niner. Like them too, he had learned of the silver from the three scalp hunters in California. Unlike them, he had hung with the scalp hunters until he got definite directions. Then, years later, he had gone down to Parral in the state of Chihuahua, thrown in with a mining man named Goff, and actually located the ledge, assays of specimen ore showing it to be exceedingly rich. He and his pardner had not denounced the property, however, or made any other move towards developing it. Chaotic political conditions in Mexico and the wild Indians that still terrorized the territory had decided them to wait.

"All this, in great detail, Fancher had imparted to

[273]

Heath and Burris in Eagle Pass, where chance had brought them together. How Fancher came to be in Eagle Pass makes a part of the story.

"Six or eight months back he had engaged by letter to meet Goff, his pardner in locating the scalp hunters' silver, at Saint Louis. There they expected to buy machinery, make other arrangements for developing the mine, and then proceed to Chihuahua. Fancher arrived in Saint Louis a few days ahead of the date set for the meeting. While he was waiting, news broke of the Sierra Mojada silver strike. He concluded at once that somebody had beat him to Scalp Hunters' Ledge. Sierra Mojada was at that time just a name of a mountain not on any procurable maps. It wasn't known whether it lay in Coahuila or Chihuahua, the line between those states not having been determined. The maps now show it to be east of the Chihuahua line. Fancher burned to get to Mexico at once, but he continued to wait for his pardner. A week dragged by, and not a word from Goff. As a matter of fact, Goff was dead and buried with three or four bullet holes through his heart, though Fancher didn't find this out until he got down to Chihuahua.

"While he paced the lobby floor in the Saint Louis hotel, he imparted his worries to the young clerk, McNeill. Finally he decided to wait no longer but take the railroad for San Antonio, go from there to Eagle Pass by stage, and find out definitely whether the Sierra Mojada discovery was his silver or not. He asked Mc-Neill to go with him, promising to 'take care of him.' In Eagle Pass he learned from Heath and Burris that Sierra Mojada was away too far east for the scalp hunter silver. He wanted men he could trust to go on with him; he was set on opening up the mine.

"For a time I reserved considerable doubt about Fancher and his plausible story. I thought he might be after working Captain Burris for money. Heath had nothing. That may explain his acting as cook. Nevertheless, I joined in with Will Smith on the deal, our percentage of the silver to be settled later. Fancher wasn't turning loose any directions to Scalp Hunters' Ledge — not yet. The plan was to go to El Paso and then south.

"We finally arrived at El Paso — just a little Mexican town then. Fancher seemed to be waiting for something — I've never known what. My suspicions grew. He wasn't as sound a man physically as he looked to be. After we'd hung around town for a week, camping by an irrigation ditch, Fancher came into camp one evening pretty excited.

" 'Boys,' he said, 'I'm being watched. I've got to get out of here quick.'

"It wouldn't do for all of us to enter Mexico in a

body, he said. His proposal was that he and Burris leave horseback for Chihuahua City that night, and that the rest of us follow in a day or two, bringing along plenty of ammunition and saddles. He told us to just stay on the old Chihuahua Road until we reached the springs called Ojo de Agua, a hundred miles or so south of El Paso, and there to halt and await a message from him. It seemed to me a desperate thing for those two old men to set out alone on a two-hundred-and-fifty-mile ride through Indian-infested desert. Fancher was a heavy man. He had a trouble that made horseback riding very painful. In fact, I did not see how he could ride at all. When he and Burris set out about midnight, they were riding horses that would get them there and that Fancher, not Burris, had paid for. I decided there might be something to him. At the same time, I considered our plan, to go to a spring in the middle of a desert and there wait until somebody told us to go somewhere else, a wild goose chase. Well, it wasn't tame geese I was after in those days.

"We got the wagons through the sand dunes and then struck the open rolling country, taking it slow and keeping our water barrels full, except when we had to empty them at dry camps. Fancher and Burris had been gone over a week when, late one afternoon, we saw a Mexican rider approaching from the south. He said he was looking for an *Americano* named Heath. Then he delivered a letter addressed to Heath. It was from Fancher and, without explanation, merely directed us to stay at Ojo de Agua until further advised. We were near the spring at the time — a famous watering place on the ranch of millions of acres belonging to Don Luis Terrazas. We waited and waited. One day some of the Terrazas men, well armed, tied in with a small band of Apaches at a spring not far from the one where we were camped. We got our hand into the shooting, but it was a one-sided fracas. We couldn't eat nearly enough antelope meat to keep me occupied hunting. Ten or twelve days passed, and still no message. We were too restless to wait longer and so headed on south for Chihuahua City. That very day we met old Captain Burris. He had plenty to tell.

"He and Fancher had made it into Chihuahua City without troubles except for Burris's going blind, temporarily, from a sand storm. Then Fancher became very sick, too sick, he claimed, to ride any farther. He explained that a noted surgeon in San Francisco had once operated on him, restoring him to soundness. Now he was bound to get back to this surgeon. Accordingly he had taken a stage for some point in the Sierra Madre. From there he was going by mule, or maybe a mule-carried litter, across to the Gulf of California and there get a boat for San Francisco. On the way down to Chihuahua City and before he left, Fancher had talked very freely about the silver. The sum and substance of his final talk to Burris was this:

" 'You have proven yourself to me a just and true man. I trust you now to go on and denounce the mine in our name. I will give you directions to the ledge. Start from Ojo de Agua and ride towards the range of mountains to the west. It runs from northwest to southeast. Cross it. Fifteen miles or so away, running in the same general direction, is a second range of mountains. Cross it. A third range parallels these two ranges. Cross it. Now ride on towards the southeast, following the valley between the third range of mountains crossed and a fourth range that must not be crossed. After riding for three or four hours you will see the color of the fourth range of mountains change to a whitish chalk. Cutting in from this limestone is a canyon with walls straight up and down. Ride up this canyon. You will find great boulders littering its floor, and your way through them will be difficult. After a while the canyon will widen out and the wall on the south side will grow less and less steep until you find yourself on a kind of sloping mesa. On this mesa you will see madroño trees. South and east of the trees you will see the outcrop of silver ore, a ledge running for a long distance. In the

gulch, or canyon, below is a fine spring, the water from which soon sinks in the gravel and rocks.'

"Burris had a kind of map that Fancher had drawn. He didn't have a doubt of Fancher's word. We turned back to Ojo de Agua and camped. Captain Burris, McNeill and I were to scout out the country, Heath and Will Smith to guard the wagon and animals.

"We three picked our mules to ride and traveled light, taking only guns, some food in morrals, canteens, and one blanket each. Passing over the three ranges of mountains as directed, we came into a valley that we followed up in a southeast direction, the drainage in that section being towards the north. We saw the change in formation to our right, and headed towards some high white bluffs that proved to mark the entrance into a canyon. It was a bear for roughness, the canyon floor being in places simply packed with enormous boulders. There wasn't even a deer trail to follow. Finally we got up to where the left side of the canyon was a fairly easy slope that planed off into a mesa, and there stood the madroño trees, mixed with oaks.

"The showdown was coming pretty soon. Without saying anything, we all reined back to give Burris the lead — though I'll say right here he wasn't a natural leader of men. He kept the lead until we were about out of the wooded area. The madroño has a reddish bark that peels off like parchment, leaving the bole and limbs of the tree slick and cool to the touch. I don't know any tree, excepting an aspen or beech maybe, that's so easy to carve into. It's squatty and often so crooked as to look contorted.

"Well, almost at the southeast point of the woods, Burris stopped by a particularly big and particularly crooked madroño, the bole of which was hidden by underbrush. It was rough ground all around. He kinder leaned over and then said, 'There she is!'

"Calling that outcrop of silver a ledge is hardly accurate. It was more of a dike. It bulged up under that tree as plain as the nose on your face, once you got a good look at it. The tree had three old bullet holes in it. According to Burris, Fancher's story was that the scalp hunters killed an Apache under it, while he was dodging behind it, and then when they went up to take his scalp they saw the silver. The tree ought to have had a cross or somebody's initials on it or something like that, I guess. But it didn't. All it had was three bullet pits, and it hadn't grown much since the bullets entered it. It was an old, old tree but still strong. The ore looked like silver to me. Captain Burris, who really knew minerals, pronounced it silver beyond a doubt. I'm satisfied that a geologist could trace that dike, or outcrop.

"All we could do was look. We did manage to pry and knock off a few samples with spurs and butcher-knife, but we hadn't brought a pick or any other kind of tool. We had come merely to reconnoiter. The only thing to do was go back to camp at Ojo de Agua. Before we left, we watered at the spring. I kept expecting to find some bones of the Apaches killed between the water and the madroño marking the silver. Coyotes no doubt gnawed the carcasses and scattered the bones. The country was so desolate and empty that I could well believe no human beings but stray Apaches and Fancher with his pardner Goff had laid eyes on the spring or the madroños since the scalp hunters passed that way thirty years before.

"The night after we got back to Ojo de Agua, we almost had a quarrel. Burris, as the man who had brought the directions from Fancher, claimed a third interest in the mine, another third belonging, of course, to Fancher, thus leaving only a third to be divided among McNeill, Heath, Will Smith and myself. We four were not at all suited. Finally it was agreed to put the division off until the papers were drawn up. The thing to do now was to put up a claim notice at the ledge and then go to Chihuahua City and legally make the denouncement, which would include surveying the claims.

"The next day the same three of us who made the first trip set out again, fully equipped with guns, ammunition, provisions and tools, a pack mule carrying most of the stuff. As I remember, the ledge is about two days' ride from Ojo de Agua. We crossed two of the mountain ranges and then halted for a late noon. We stopped at a spot protected by boulders and rock walls opening out on a well-grassed little plain. After making coffee and drinking it, we all lay down in the shade for a little siesta.

"I had my hat over my face so as to shut out the fierce light and was dozing off when all at once something aroused me. I think it was the sudden ceasing of the horses to graze. A grazing horse makes a kind of musical noise cropping grass and grinding it, and men out, with their lives depending on horses, often notice that music or the absence of it. Anyhow, when I raised up, I saw every animal with head up and ears pointed to the range of mountains we had last crossed. I looked too and saw a thin, stringy cloud of dust.

" 'Indians,' I yelled.

"We had plenty of time to prepare. We gathered our horses and equipment into the protected *rincón*, or pocket. Somehow I did not feel uneasy. I had confidence in our ability to protect ourselves. McNeill felt the same way. We had enough ammunition to supply a company of rangers; we had a little water in our canteens. But old man Burris was panic-stricken. He was for surrendering before he got a good view of the oncoming riders.

"As they drew near, we saw they were Mexicans and not Indians. There were about twenty-five of them. They demanded a surrender.

" 'Surrender, hell,' McNeill yelled.

"I was with him. At that time there were men still living in Texas who had killed Mexicans to avenge the Goliad Massacre, who as members of the Mier Expedition had drawn for the white beans of life against the black beans of death, and who as members of the Santa Fe Expedition had seen their comrades, after surrendering, shot down and have their ears cut off. For a Texan to surrender to Mexicans was regarded as suicide.

" 'Why do you want us?' I asked the Mexicans.

" 'We are troops and we arrest you for smuggling goods into Mexico,' they replied.

"While we were talking, old man Burris slipped out on the open and was walking to them with hands up. I never saw anything like what he did. He must have gone crazy.

" 'What shall we do?' I said to McNeill.

" 'Well, Burris is in their hands. If we shoot, they will kill him,' McNeill answered.

" 'All right, we'll give up then,' I agreed.

"We gave up. The Mexicans, of course, took all our stuff, then mounted us on our horses and set out. Among them I noticed a man, Pedro García, I had come to know at Sierra Mojada; his son was in the company also. During the afternoon I managed to ride up alongside Pedro and exact from him a promise to get word to the American consul at Chihuahua City. So far as I know, the consul did not help us any; Pedro's good word did. But for Pedro our bodies would very likely have been left to bleach out in the mountains instead of being delivered into the jail at Parral.

"At length we were released, penniless, stripped. The

two men waiting for us at Ojo de Agua had, as I later learned, given us up for dead and gone back to Texas. While in prison I contracted what developed into slow fever; it was many weeks before I was strong enough to travel northward. When I got back home, I had been gone nearly a year.

"Since coming out of Chihuahua I have never heard a word concerning Fancher. Perhaps he did not live to reach San Francisco; undoubtedly he has been dead many, many years now. Heath and Burris soon passed off the scene. My dear friend Will Smith had a large family and became, like me, a settled man; he has been dead more than twenty years now. What became of McNeill, I do not know. Very likely I am the only living man who has seen the silver ledge discovered by the scalp hunters. I have no idea what became of the puny samples of ore we got with butcherknife and spurs. In a kind of day-dreaming way I have often planned to go back, but have never made the start."

Not many years after relating this story to me, John C. Beasley joined the other silver hunters on the yon side of the Great Divide. Times have changed in Mexico as everywhere else, but there are plenty of places in the Sierra Madre that have not changed much since the scalp hunters in 1849 rode away from that bulging outcrop of silver under a gnarled madroño tree to take a chance at gold on and on far beyond.

El Naranjal

EL NARANJAL

Only a little less famous than Tayopa is the Lost Naranjal Mine. It appeals to my imagination more because of the ancient hacienda and the orange grove — *naranjal* — associated with it. It was owned by one of those Spanish grandees who would not deign to shake hands with his manager but would offer him only the tip of his cane to shake and who, when visited by a bishop, paved the path between his house and the church with silver for his pontifical excellence to sweep his robes over. Nobody can understand the tradition of El Naranjal unless he remembers how, beginning about 1810, native Mexico rose up against the grandee class, extirpated them, and then for years and years remained a chaos in which fine haciendas reverted to the desert and rich mines were filled with water and debris.

El Naranjal is on the floor of one of those Grand Canyons, called *barrancas,* cutting down from the heights of the Sierra Madre to the West Coast. The bottom of a *barranca* may be a rock-walled millrace; it may be a narrow bench of tropical luxuriance. Most of the gold-dreaming detectives who seek El Naranjal have placed it more or less — with emphasis upon the *more* — out from the line dividing the states of Durango and Sinaloa. It is supposed to be in the country of the Tepehuane Indians — an enormous country. Some say the Naranjal got its name from the fact that its gold, occurring in conjunction with silver, was found in orange-like balls. Others tell of oranges floating down a certain river from the *naranjal*, which, though un-located, still flourishes. The big hacienda that was once so thriving beside the orange grove is enchanted now, they say, as proven by the far-away sound of bells — always, always, far-away — that a few persons have heard at high noon, mid-afternoon and evening Angelus time.

A British consul who stayed on the trail of El Naran-jal for many, many years told me that in the church records of Guadalajara he found proof of the mine's having produced millions during the seventeenth cen-tury. At Mazatlan I once met a German assayer who had a piece of evidence hard to ignore. This was the reproduction of a road sign found by an American prospector nearly forty years ago. He had for a long time been prospecting in a canyon-jungle country, where water washes dumps away and caves-in tunnels. Then, beside the traces of a long disused trail, he noticed the remains of a cross beside a rock. The rock was split, but on the face of it he saw some weathered lettering. With much patience he worked out the inscription until it was clear. It read:

†

Departemento
de
Caminos
Camino a Las Minas
de Arco
y
Naranjal

In other words, the sign was put up by the Department of Roads, saying, "Road to the Mines of Arco and Naranjal." One of the traditions of the Naranjal is that it was within reach of another mine called the Juana Arco — Joan of Arc.

Traveling by mule — the only way there is to travel, unless an airship is chartered — from Durango to Mazatlan, one tops the very crest almost of a mountain called Huehuente, the "Go-Between," ten thousand feet above sea level. There the rare and gorgeous imperial woodpecker still cries his wild startling cry, which can be heard easily a mile away, and flashes his gorgeous colors. While I was halted enthralled by a pair of these astounding birds, my *mozo*, honest and stately "Don" Pedro, swept his long arm towards a *barranca*, the cliffs of which could be seen a vast and untravelable distance away to the northwest, and said, "In that direction lies El Naranjal." Two days later we came to a river, vised in a profound gorge, flowing out of that "direction." Following down the river, the trail often had to corkscrew a thousand feet above it. The trail came to the great Tayoltita mine, near which one may enter a tunnel wherein the cruel and powerful Zambrano had dungeons, yet visible, for holding his slave peons at night. Then the trail threads through tunnels, just ample enough to admit a loaded mule, that have in the manner of railroad tunnels been blasted out of solid rock, or it hangs on rock platforms straight above the ribbon of water twisting below. The outlandishly crested urracas shriek their outlandish cries, flocks of guacamayo parrots fill the air with unearthly noises, and the traveler may well imagine that in one direction or another the river in that gash — which, once in, he may no more leave than the water can — must lead to a mystery that no amount of exploration could ever uncover.

But the nearest I have been to Naranjal was far away from it. The man was one of those characters found only in the land of the Sierra Madre: half-Mexicanized through long residence in the country and wholly naturalized through its liquors and *no le hace* — "it doesn't matter after all" — ways of life; always threatening to leave it, yet never leaving; always expecting to strike it rich, yet never driving the pick in quite far enough.

"I have seen El Naranjal," he said.

Had he said, "The burro is lazy," his tone would have been no more accented. Yet for his listener, at least, the statement was amazing. There followed a silence, not dramatic or strained with suspense, but easy, as belongs to the shade in a little Mexican patio. Then a bottle and those long black cigarettes sweetened with cinnamon.

"Yes," the man went on,[1] "I have seen El Naranjal. It happened this way. I had been prospecting all summer around an old pueblo away north of Durango and was coming in for the Sixteenth of September fiesta. About sundown on the first day of travel, my little mule pointed his ears towards a lone Mexican rancho just off the trail and nickered. It was the first habitation we had seen in many hours. As the mule halted in front of the log house, a white-haired man came out and I asked if I could sleep there. He lived alone, I

---

[1] The tale the man told is taken by arrangement with the Appleton-Century Company, New York, from Wallace Gillpatrick's richly stored book, too little known and long out of print, *The Man Who Likes Mexico*, New York, 1911, pages 54-64.

found, and as the trail was seldom traveled, he seemed rather glad to see me. I had a quart of Scotch whisky I had been saving, and when we had made a supper on beans and tortillas, I got it out. After a few pulls, he became exceedingly friendly. The only strangers that ever go into that part of the country are mining men; so he knew my business. He turned the talk on old mines, and finally told me he knew where there was a very rich one, with a ruined hacienda.

"He said he saw it during a war. He didn't know what war, but it was probably during the French intervention of the Sixties. The Government was sending soldiers into the mountains after recruits. He took what few cattle he had and drove them over the mountains and down the west slope. An old trail brought him to the bottom of a deep, deep canyon, and there he came upon an abandoned hacienda. Oranges were still growing around it. Close by was a mine that had been worked extensively, and on the dump he picked up a piece of rock containing chunks of gold as yellow as the oranges. I questioned him more closely. He said the orange trees were very, very old. He stayed in the canyon half a year, not seeing a human being the whole time, before venturing to come back to his ranch.

"I felt satisfied he had seen the lost Naranjal. I asked

him if he would take me there. He said he had never been back and that the place was at 'the tail end of the world.' When I pressed him further, he became very reticent; so the subject was dropped.

"The next morning I waited anxiously for him to refer to it again, but he said never a word. My experience with Indians had taught me never to try forcing their hand. The old fellow had treated me well, and as I was about to leave, I gave him the flask. It was elaborately embossed and still had a little whisky in it. His eyes glistened with delight and he went and put it carefully inside an ancient chest made of rawhide that stood in the corner. Returning, he handed me, without speaking, a piece of rock. Instinctively I knew it was the rock he had picked up on the ore-dump by the orange grove. I held it to the light and saw gold nuggets, as big as the end of my little finger.

"I looked at the old man and waited for him to speak. Instead, he took my arm and led me into the corral. Then, pointing to the mountains, he asked if I saw a peak that looked like a big *piloncillo* (conical loaf of sugar). I judged it to be a long day's ride away.

" 'I see it clearly,' I answered.

"He was silent for a time, as if he were considering whether to tell more. Then he said, 'The trail I followed crosses the sierra at that point.'

"Then he was silent again. At last he concluded, 'If you wish to see the old mine, I will conduct you as far as the peak and put you on the right trail. Beyond, I will not go. The trail is dim, dim, but there is a trail. The other side is the country of bears and tigers. You must go well armed and with provisions for a week, two weeks.'

"Impressed as I was by what this man had told me, for there could be no doubt of his honesty, I was in no position to profit by it, immediately at least. I was alone, five days from Durango, my only chance of raising money for an outfit and equipment. I knew, however, I would never know a day's rest until I returned. I cautioned the old man not to mention the mine to anyone else. He looked at me gravely and replied, 'I was young when I saw the oranges. You are the first man to whom I have ever spoken of the discovery. But do not wait too long to come back. The years are adding themselves.'

"When I arrived in Durango, I was notified that the men I had been working for did not need my services any longer. I tried in vain to interest several mining men in El Naranjal. They all heard my story through, but those with ability to act invariably had too many irons in the fire to set out on any such wild goose chase, as they termed my proposal. I was driven to a job that cut me off from all exploration and that paid little beyond my necessities.

"Years went by. I never forgot the old Indian's story and the sight I had had of the gold-plugged rock from El Naranjal. Yet I could never quite see my way clear to make the long trip. Yes, I am a drinking man, a heavy one at times, like nearly all the old stagers. Often the money that might have taken me over the trail to El Naranjal and a fortune went into a spree. Finally it got so that when I told my story, people only laughed.

"Ten years went by before I saw my chance. I was working for some rich Americans, sinking a shaft in a place that I judged to be four days' ride from the old Indian's rancho. I had about twenty peons under me and was in full control. The lead we were following was petering out and further work seemed foolish. The Naranjal kept haunting me. Plans for going after it went on working in my mind like yeast. One night in a dream I saw, as plain as I can still see the old Indian pointing towards the peak, the ruined hacienda down in the canyon with the orange trees growing about it. The next day I picked out four of my best men, laid the others off, packed a good supply of grub and my bedding on two pack mules, and hit the trail. Of course I did wrong in abandoning, without consulting my employers, the work I had been set to do. I had El Naranjal on my brain. Yet I had no doubt of success, and I planned to let my employers, who unknown to themselves were grubstaking me, share the results. My only anxiety was about the old Indian. Was he still alive?

"I am a good man of the camp. Only rarely have I been 'northed,' as the Mexicans say of one who has lost his directions. After I had pushed ahead four days, I still knew I was coursing correctly, but I began to wonder if I had missed the right trail. Then about sundown I saw the familiar rancho, and the memory of a mule's nicker came into my mind. My heart was beating fast. A middle-aged man, too young to be my friend, came out of the house. He was the old fellow's brother though. He said his brother had been dead for several years. He could not remember how many. We were hospitably invited to spend the night, the peons sleeping outside. During the course of the evening I touched on the subject of lost mines, but my host professed the densest ignorance regarding them. At last I asked him point blank if his brother had never told him of the oranges and the gold. I added that he had not only told me, but offered to guide me to the place.

"For a second he eyed me suspiciously. Then, going

to the old rawhide chest, which was still in its place in the corner, he took from it a black flask elaborately embossed and, holding it up before me, asked if it were mine. For a moment I was puzzled. Not once during all those years had I remembered the flask itself, the whisky without reference to the container having been what I considered of value to the Indian as well as to myself. I now replied that the flask had once been mine but that I had given it to his brother.

"At that the man became, for an Indian, voluble. He said his brother had always looked for my return and had at the very close of his life instructed him, in case I did come, to go with me to the cone-shaped mountain and show me the old trail. He agreed to go with me the next morning. It was a long night. We left early.

"Just a little before sundown we reached the crest of the mountain. My guide got off his mule and began scanning the westward slope. At length he gave a satisfied grunt, and, parting the tall grass with his hands, pointed to a faint trace on the ground leading downhill. I was to follow that trail two or three days — *mas ó menos* (more or less) — he said, and then I should see the hacienda below me. He then put out his hand. Greatly surprised, I pressed him to spend the night with us, but he steadfastly refused. With a backward glance that had in it, I thought, something of dread, he said, 'May you go with God,' and disappeared in the thickening shadows.

"We had a dry camp, but the water in our canteens was sufficient for our needs. I knew we should strike water farther down. We started as soon as it was light, and then began one of the hardest jobs I have ever undertaken. It is not always a simple matter in rough mountains to keep on a trail even in fairly regular use. When it comes to keeping on one that has not been traveled at all for a generation, the keenest and most unremitting observation is required. But a trail among rocks always leaves a scar. Sometimes we lost this one and were an hour threshing around in the brush before we picked it up again, usually at a distance, where the scar would show up more plainly than near at hand. Mules are often expert at keeping a trail, but here ours were at more of a loss than we were. In places we had to cut our way with machetes through dense growth. Sundown found us on a bare ledge of rocks where the trail disappeared. There was nothing to do but camp.

"At daylight we were hunting for the lost trace. The men had declared repeatedly that we were at the end of it, when I discovered it, doubling on itself and leading into the brush again. I sent two men ahead with machetes to clear a path, while the rest of us followed slowly with the animals. The second night found us apparently no nearer the goal. We were still descending the mountain; on every hand stretched the limitless chaparral. I have been in lonely places, but never one like that. The old Indian had talked of bears and jaguars. Here there was absolutely not one sign of life, not a bird's twitter in the brush; not an animal track beside the pool of water, in an otherwise dry arroyo, where we had stopped. The only animal life we had seen during two days was an occasional buzzard, sailing overhead.

"The men showed themselves very downcast, and after supper one of them came and asked me to turn back. He said his companions were all *muy triste* (very sad) and 'afraid we were going to the death.' I asked him why they were afraid. He replied because the buzzards had followed us for two days. I told him to make ready for an early start and assured him, quoting the guide as authority, that we should reach the old hacienda in one more day. Then I rolled myself in my blankets — and remembered the old darky story about the buzzard awaiting the will of God.

"When I awoke, it was not yet light, but I felt that I was alone. I called out, but there was no reply. The cowards, satisfied that I would not turn back no matter how much they urged, had deserted me in the darkness. At daylight I found they had taken most of the provisions. I cursed them until I was tired out, swearing with every oath that I would never give up until I had reached the mine. If I failed before I reached it, the buzzards were welcome to my carcass. Then I started again, hewing when necessary with a machete luckily left behind. I kept on all day, not even stopping to eat. I had about decided to camp and wait for another day, when I suddenly came to a part of the slope that seemed a wide ledge of sandstone. It was almost devoid of vegetation, and here the trail was sharply defined, being worn deep in the formation. I determined to push on, relying on my mule to keep the trail.

"It was now so dark I could not see four feet ahead. The mule seemed nervous and several times stood stock-still. Each time she stopped, I would get off and grope about in the darkness to make sure I was still on the trail. I had just gotten in the saddle and had ridden perhaps five rods farther, when she came to a sudden standstill, snorted, and began to tremble. I urged her forward, but she reared, whirled, and tried to bolt up the mountain. I headed her back downhill, got down and again assured myself we were on the trail in the standstone formation, and once more urged her forward. She took a few steps, stopped again, and showed every sign of extreme terror.

"Dismounting once more, I took a step forward, at the same time clasping the bridle reins in one hand and keeping the other on her neck. One foot went into space. The stout reins, my firm grasp, and the mule's jerking back saved my life. I had three or four matches left. I determined to save them for hard times, and to wait for daylight to reveal what sort of jump-off I had come to. I retreated a short distance, tied the mule short to a shrub, and fell into the sleep of utter exhaustion.

"When I awoke, the sun was shining. I had indeed come to the end of the trail. The void beyond me to the west made me feel faint even before I edged to the brink. As I now gazed, fear and wonder and incomprehension, to say nothing of being absolutely halted, all appalled me. The fear was from the past, the headlong death barely missed in the darkness. I had been above and had gone down into deep *barrancas* of the Sierra Madre, but never had I come abruptly upon one like this. The bottom still lay in shadows, though the rising sun was already gleaming on the cliffs and pillars of the opposite wall. The ancient trail could not have had as its objective this impassable brink amid utter desolation, overlooking utter space.

Originally the trail must have gone on down. The mountain appeared to have been sliced off as sheer as a loaf of bread cut half in two. Hanging over the edge, I could see straight down for thousands of feet. The bluff seemed to be perpendicular, without slope. I estimated the depth to be around four thousand feet. The floor of the canyon must have been a mile across, a very rough, broken kind of badlands country. The river was near the far edge of the floor. As far up and as far down as I could see, the walls on both sides of the *barranca* were sheer bluffs.

"When the sun got a little higher, a shining, broken line of silver caught my eye — a river, of course. And there close beside it was a clump of bright green foliage, the sheen on it different from that on any other growth along the canyon bottom. Back in and beyond these trees — oranges — I made out patches of white that could be nothing else than the stone walls of some hacienda.

"Yes, yonder was El Naranjal, the Naranjal of a thousand stories of vast fortune, the Naranjal that my old Indian friend had descended to and from it brought a rock studded with golden nuggets. I wondered if, only a half-century or so before, he had found the trail zigzagging down a steep slope now annihilated by nature, or if he had come to the brink as I had come

I reached the rancho, only to find it deserted. I located a little corn in the house, parched it and ground it up on a *metate*. With water it was mighty good and gave me strength. I rested a day, making a supply of tortillas. Then I set out for Durango. I was lucky in falling in with some muleteers freighting over a trail that mine entered. They had plenty to eat, and for a part of the distance they gave me a mule to ride.

"Upon reaching the city, I sent a full account of my experiences to my employers. I doubted whether they would believe me, and I felt low anyhow. While I was waiting for instructions, I went on a spree. It ended in an attack of fever. When I came to my senses, two letters, both from my employers, were handed me. The first one said that my report warranted further investigation and that I should come at once to outfit for it. The second, dated two weeks later, said that my goings on had been learned of and fully considered and that no further relations with me were desired.

"I told my story over and over, but no man with means would take any stock in it. Again I was forced to delay arrival at El Naranjal. I shall have one more try at it, though. This time I shall have men with me who will stay, and I will have enough ropes along to let myself down into the *barranca* at some descendable place. I will hunt a place up and down from where

Tom Lea

El Naranjal

the trail ends. Not even in that vast lost world will El Naranjal be forever lost."

This is the story of the man who saw El Naranjal. Meantime the ancient hacienda sleeps peacefully on among the orange trees, and sometimes a golden orange is rolled by wind or water into the stream and floats away from the place of gold still waiting to be recovered. Lure on, O Naranjal, of the golden oranges and the orange gold! As with the lover prefigured on the Grecian urn, yearning forever towards the maiden forever fixed there out of reach, so — perhaps — with the dreamers and seekers of El Naranjal.

Bold Lover, never, never canst thou kiss,
　　Though winning near the goal — yet, do not grieve;
She cannot fade, though thou hast not thy bliss,
　　For ever wilt thou love, and she be fair!

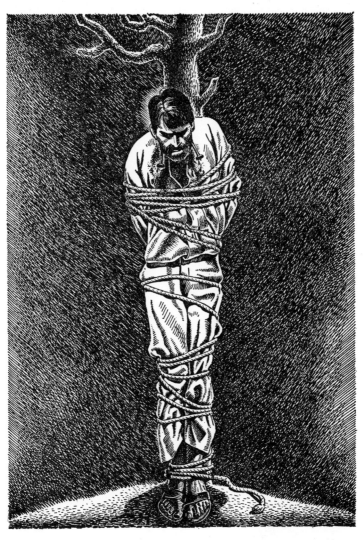

Pedro Loco

PEDRO LOCO

Pedro Loco, some say, was one of old Victorio's Apaches before a Mexican woman cut him off. Others say he was as Mexican as anybody, a descendant of the peon that the Conde de Majalca left to guard his property when the War of Mexican Independence ran all the Spaniards out of the country.

Whatever his antecedents, no particular interest or property had been attached to his person until one day in 1890 when he appeared at the Banco Nacional de Mexico in Chihuahua City with a few flat-cut emeralds, some jewelry that might have adorned a holy churchman or a holy image, a small chunk of crude gold, and one of the old-time bars of silver weighing 2000 ounces — twice as much as the regulation bar has weighed since Spain lost Mexico. The banker struck a bargain and was curious; Pedro took the money and was silent. Within a few months he was back again with another parcel of treasure stuff. The banker paid for it, was more curious, and set spies to watch Pedro.

Pedro did not come to him again, but there were other buyers and Pedro sold to them. Traffic in bullion and stuff out of old hoards is still common enough in Chihuahua City. The banker's spies learned nothing.

Apache Gold and Yaqui Silver

Before long, people began calling Pedro "Don." He set up an establishment. It was not so magnificent as it was ample, its adobe walls and patios squandering over a whole square of ground. It had to be ample to accommodate all the uncles, aunts, cousins unto the remotest degree and even the kin of godfathers and godmothers that settled down on Don Pedro and his wife. It took money to keep such a household in corn and frijoles, and during the dark of the moon at irregular intervals Don Pedro continued to bring in modest amounts of silver to barter.

His movements were more and more watched. It was daylight knowledge that when he left Chihuahua City, he went northwest to Sacramento. Thence his movements blurred and faded out, as if he had turned into a "fool" (Mearns) quail that squats unseen against a rock in open view. All interested parties, however, were sure that Don Pedro went on from Sacramento into the mountain region not far distant called the "Victorino," a name that memorializes one of the strongholds of Victorio of the Apaches. In the Victorino, Conde de Majalca had his mine, enormously rich in silver output, before the War of Independence ended him. It is told that he used to make a trip to Mexico City once a year, carrying four hundred bars of silver, his guard, servants and muleteers numbering four hundred persons. The little village of Majalca, in the Victorino, bears his name. Before he was killed on the long road to a ship that would sail him over the sea, he had hidden not only his own fine possessions but the riches of the Chihuahua Cathedral in a cave near his mine, or in a chamber of the mine itself.

Now, among those who dogged Don Pedro, trying to find the store from which he got his silver, was one Carlos Avalos, a "tiger" of political notoriety. By many ways he brought pressure to bear against Don Pedro. He persecuted him through other politicians. He cajoled him, set traps for him, played the bloodhound himself. One time he waylaid Don Pedro in the Sacramento Canyon and there attempted by brute force to make him talk. Don Pedro remained calm and silent. Avalos tied him and tortured him, but the Indian in him was adamant.

"Then, damn you," concluded Avalos, "I'll fix you so you can't talk even if you want to."

Pedro was pinioned arms and legs, helpless. His torturer had two forty-penny nails. He drove them into the jaws of the silent man, one on either side of his face, nailing the upper to the lower jaw. He rode off leaving Pedro tied and nailed. A wood-carrier came along with his burro and rescued Pedro. He recovered, but to the end of his days he carried deep scars in his face and was *"un poco loco"* — a little crazy. Henceforth he was Pedro Loco. But he was not too loco still to go in secret and come back in secret with gold and silver and jewelry and the flat-cut emeralds. And he was not too loco to keep his jaws closed.

Once, however, once only, he relented. He had a very dear friend who was in desperate need and who was very deferential. This friend was Felipe Jimenez.

"The first day," Felipe used to tell, "we rode our mules up the canyon a way from Sacramento and camped. When we ate our supper, the wild turkeys were gobbling around us in every direction. About dark Pedro Loco turned his mule loose, saying that it would go home by itself and that from now on he would go afoot and guide my mule. We rode on for three hours maybe, and I knew we were getting into the mountains of the Rancho Guerachic" — another name for Majalca.

"At a certain place Pedro Loco blindfolded me fast and hard. On foot he followed behind my mule, driving it. Of course the canyon twists and the wind in it shifts and changes too. But I was keeping very alert and noted every change of direction. I was sure that we left the Sacramento Canyon and turned up a canyon that cuts in from the north. We did not ride more than an hour before we stopped. I heard the sounds of rocks. Then Pedro Loco told me to get down. He led me over some boulders. For a short distance we crawled. When he took the blindfold off me, we were in a cave and two sotol stalks were burning to light it. It was not the light that almost blinded me; it was the heap of precious stones, of gold, most of all, of silver bullion, and also of jewelry. There were beautiful crosses and fine plate, candlesticks, and holy vessels.

" 'Help yourself,' Pedro Loco said. I did. Then when my pockets were full, he put the blind on me, tighter than before. I crawled again. I heard the sound of loose rocks — very, very dim the sound was. My mule went forward. I knew we were not returning over the same route. My brain was not blind like my eyes. I began fraying the blanket I wore and dropping the shreds. I was marking the trail to come back over. I felt on my face the cold breeze of dawn. We kept traveling, Pedro Loco close at my mule's heels and I dropping here and there a shred of the blanket.

"At length we halted. I heard a dog bark. It must have been a dog at the Rancho Guerachic, for there is no other ranch in that part of the Victorino.

" 'Get down,' Pedro Loco said. These were the first words he had spoken since leaving the cave. I did not

like their tone. I obeyed. I could smell the dawn. When the blind came off, I saw that we were on a mountain. Pedro Loco was standing there with his hands full of woolen shreds.

" 'Here is your blanket,' he said. 'Your wife can weave it back together.' Then he gave me a kick. I felt too cheap to kick back. 'You cannot betray me,' he said. 'Go home!'

"I left him standing there and rode back to Chihuahua City. I sent to San Antonio, Texas, for my brothers to come and help me get the wealth. For five years we sought. All I know is that Pedro Loco showed me the treasure. He told me he had located it while he was a warrior with Victorio."

In the fall of 1908 Victor Lieb and Bill Adams, two American mining men who had been in Chihuahua for years and were familiar with the facts and traditions connected with Pedro Loco and his secret treasure, determined to exert superior Anglo-American intelligence and find the wealth. They disguised their purpose by getting permits to prospect for minerals in the Victorino. Lieb sent for a bloodhound out of the stock employed by the state penitentiary in Texas. He engaged as a helper a Pima Indian noted for his trailing ability. The dog proved to be marvelously keen of scent and was soon taught to trail silently on the leash.

November passed and December was passing. Without doubt Pedro Loco would make a trip out before Christmas. Lieb and Adams had their camp above Sacramento in the mouth of the canyon gorge. On the evening of December 20, Pedro Loco rode up on his mule, saluted the two Americans in a friendly manner, drank some coffee, and rode on. At dark they followed, the bloodhound silently straining on the leash. The trail turned out of the main canyon and up a box canyon cutting in from the north — the route that the blindfolded Felipe was so sure of.

It was pitch-dark. About half a mile up this side

[317]

canyon the bloodhound suddenly ceased to trail, whined in fear, bolted back the way he had come, and jerked with such violence on the thong, which Lieb for safety's sake had tied around his waist, that he broke it. Among the rocks and trees hidden in the pitchy darkness the winds were howling. Lieb and Adams turned back also. They found the dog in camp. Impatiently they awaited daylight. When light dawned, they took the bloodhound and the expert Pima trailer and set out. At the mouth of the box canyon, the bloodhound refused to go farther. The Pima proceeded, but soon it was apparent that instead of trailing he was merely going ahead. He could "trail a hummingbird almost," but he could not follow Pedro Loco's tracks. In places the steep slopes of the canyon wall are covered with talus. It seemed likely that Pedro Loco's cave had an entrance hidden by the talus, but not one sign of it could be found.

On Christmas Eve Lieb and Adams were back in Chihuahua City. The cold norther and the bright sun were keeping most of the permanent population of the great plaza lined up against warmth-absorbing walls. Only the blanketed and the coated could be at ease on the benches. And there in the windy sunshine the two Americanos saw Pedro Loco. He was wrapped in the blue coat he always wore and sat humped up

like an old buzzard. He looked at the pair of prospectors and grinned. They could not resist pausing
for a few words.

"I thought you'd have that fine dog with you,"
Pedro Loco said.

One thing leads to another. Living in Chihuahua City
at this time was a fairly rich and unfairly grasping
American, whose name may be indicated by the letter C.
C stands for Coyote, but I never have understood why
human beings want to libel coyotes and burros. C was,
of course, in the mining business. At various times he
had employed Victor Lieb and Bill Adams to examine
properties for him and do other work. He now came
to them saying that he wanted two or three locations
out in the Victorino country examined.

They told him they had just been prospecting in
that region, had geologized it thoroughly, and failed
to find the least indication of mineralization — no matter what the Conde de Majalca had found. But C had
some money to spend on these prospects, he said, and
was going to spend it. The pardners engaged to make
the examinations he wanted.

After they had spent about two weeks in the Victorino, C came out and agreed that further exploration was useless. The next morning the prospectors told
their *mozo* to pack up, and the outfit started back

towards Chihuahua City. But just as they were leaving camp, an oldish Indian whom Victor Lieb had once bought a panther-killing stallion from, and whom he had more than once hired as a helper, rode up. He was a Mexicanized Indian who lived away back in the mountains, where he had a few head of stock and a corn patch.

"Listen, Don Victoriano," the Indian said, "I have been wanting to see you for a long time. I know something that will interest you."

He got off his horse, pulled an old brass-bellied forty-four Winchester rifle from the deer-hide scabbard on his saddle, laid it between some rocks, and carefully sighted it.

"Look," he said.

Victor Lieb knelt and looked out beyond the line of sights.

"What do you see?" asked the Indian.

"I see the mountains."

"Yes, and you see the gap where the Arroyo de los Fresnos comes out from them. That is thirty miles from here. On a little mesa on the right-hand side of that gap is an old smelter. I have seen it. Cutting into the gap, a little beyond, is the Cañon Cantada. Vaqueros tell me that between the smelter and the mouth of the Cantada there are ruins of a mining camp. Go there and perhaps you will find something."

Lieb and his pardner had supplies enough to last three or four weeks. They had nothing to do. They decided to investigate. C wanted to be in on the chance also. He even offered to finance the expedition, and on these terms he was taken in, the three to share equally whatever might be found.

The gap of the Arroyo de los Fresnos proved to be an ideal camp — water, wood, deer all around, turkeys so gentle they would come into camp, grass belly-deep, and bear. The ruined smelter had an oak tree growing out of it that appeared to be hundreds of years old. Scattered here and there around were signs of ancient workings, but the slag about the smelter — rich slag — showed that it had not come from these workings. The problem was to find the origin of the slag.

Lieb decided to move camp from the smelter over to the ruins of the old mining camp, not a great distance off. The outfit moved, and Lieb took his horse to stake him out on a little bench. While the stake-rope was being tied, a fly or something caused the animal to stamp. The ground under the horse's hoofs sounded hollow. At this moment Lieb's eye caught sight of an outcropping vein. He yelled for the *mozo* to bring a pick. The whole camp came running.

Digging down at the exact spot where the horse had

stamped, the men very shortly struck a layer of logs. They were of the enduring juniper and were as sound as they had been the day they were buried — no doubt fully two centuries before. The rocks and soil above them all having been removed, the logs were lifted out. They covered the mouth of a shaft. Leading down into the shaft were the old-time chicken ladders, notched logs, still slick from the wear of moccasins and bare feet of Indian miners. The ladder appeared to be as sound as the juniper logs. Getting lights, ropes, and other equipment, the discoverers began to descend.

For three hundred feet they climbed down. The air was dry, and not a log of the ladder was shaky. At the bottom against a highly mineralized ledge were the remains of a fire, which had no doubt been built to heat the rock, against which water would then be dashed to make it split. Beside the charcoals were several *ollas* — earthen pots — in which water had doubtless been carried. There, too, were several *zurrones* — the bags of rawhide in which the native miners carried their burdens of ore upward, suspending them from the forehead. Truly this was a lost mine worth finding. This was the ore that had been worked at the smelter and that had left such rich slag.

Lieb drew up all the papers for denouncing the mine. He placed the papers in his instrument box, which

was never locked. They would have to be filed with
the Government. That night C left, saying he had to
get back to Chihuahua City and would meet his pardners there. He rode to a railway station not so distant
as the City, but Lieb and Adams agreed they would
load a mule with selected ore samples and go on horseback. When they reached Chihuahua City a week later
and Lieb went to get his papers to file them, they
were gone. They had been filed by C under his own
name alone.

How bad luck followed him; how the Madero Revolution came on and a pair of gringos slipped out, took
possession of the mine and were working it when
bandits surprised them with bullets; how Pancho Villa
sent the soldier of fortune Holmdahl after the bandits;
how he chased two of them horseback into the corral
at the Rancho Guerachic, jumped his horse over the
rock wall, and then with a sixshooter killed them at
such close quarters that he came out of the horseback
duel powder-burned but unwounded — all this is hardly
a part of the story.

Was the mine that Victor Lieb's horse found one of
Majalca's old mines? It was a good mine, but nobody
knows its authentic history.

"No, that was not Majalca's mine," Italian Joe as-
serted.

Apache Gold and Yaqui Silver

We were where all trails begin — in the plaza under the old bullet-pitted cathedral in Chihuahua City. Many years had passed since Pedro Loco had made his last trailless trip and been added to the legended past.

"The reason why I have been poor for thirty years," Italian Joe went on, "is that Majalca property — Pedro Loco."

I looked at Joe's sockless feet, clad in moccasins made of strings. I gave him a match to light the long cigarette he had rolled in a shuck. About every minute as we talked, one of the two hundred shine boys that belong to Chihuahua came along begging to polish my shoes.

"And I have found it," Italian Joe went on, "but not where many think it is. I found it by accident. I was camped in the Victorino, prospecting. One evening I saw a man and a boy coming down the mountain with two little mules dragging pine logs. When they saw me, they asked me where the water was. I knew then they were not of that part of the mountains. I told them. They watered their mules and made camp. That night the man and I talked of many things.

"He told me of a waybill he had seen to Majalca's mine and treasure. He described a canyon, a seep spring, a marked rock, and other points the waybill called for. I told him about old Pedro Loco. We decided to look for the mine. It was a terribly dry year. We got into the canyon that waybill called for. We came to the seep spring, but it was as dry as a bone and the ferns there were all dead. After one day of thirst we quit looking for the mine and went to looking for water. On the evening of the second day I shot a rabbit and we drank the blood. The next morning we came to the most twisted tangle of trails I have ever seen. They were centuries old, not an animal track on them. I decided to try an experiment.

"We unsaddled and turned our mules loose with drag ropes on. They headed south and struck a fast walk. We followed and before long caught up with them on a little mesa. We brought them back to the saddles and again turned them loose. They were too dry to notice the dry grass. Again they headed south. I told my pardner that we would catch the mules now, saddle them, and give them their heads. I knew they had smelled water. After traveling about a mile, I saw a rock with carving on it, but I was too thirsty to see straight or to care about anything but water. Less than an hour later the mules brought up at a little spring unmarked by a single bush or tree.

"After a while I went back to the rock. This was what was carved on its face.

"I guess you understand that the R M means REAL DE MAJALCA — Majalca's mines. We never could find the way into the storage cave though. I have been back to that region many, many times. I know Pedro Loco went there too. That is why I say the Pedro Loco Mine has kept me poor. I wish I had never seen the sign. It has kept me from profitable pursuits."

Then Italian Joe launched out to give me, for the tenth time, his intimate knowledge of Tayopa.

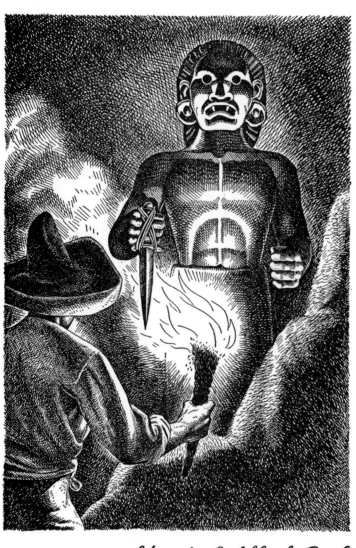

Not the Will of God

NOT THE WILL OF GOD

There were three of us — a border ranchman, his *pastor*, and myself. We had stopped at the goat camp after a long day's ride on horses. The goat-herder's fire was very cheerful as it blazed against a natural windbreak of black chaparral brush, and the odor of kid ribs roasting over it made us forget the norther.

A man is like a dog. After he has eaten he is loath to stir from warmth.

"Tomás," said the border ranchman, "I want you to tell my friend why you left Mexico for this country."

Tomás was pinching the end off a shuck cigarette filled with black-leaf "Lobo Negro" tobacco. He took a coal of fire in his fingers to light it. He adjusted the frazzled serape about his neck and shifted his squatting position so as to be a little more out of the cold wind.

"*Patrón*," he said, "I see you are taking a cough. I gathered today some of the roots of the *anacahuita*. It will be well to make you a little tea."

I had not noticed the cough. The old Mexican got a tomato can from which the top had been melted, unwrapped a flour sack that swathed the roots, broke them into the can, filled it with water, and spent fully two minutes adjusting a heap of coals to set it on.

A coyote began howling not far away.

"The coyotes," remarked the *pastor*, "have for three mornings now sung on top of the hills after sunup instead of in the valleys before the sun came out. It will rain."

Soon the tea had boiled.

"It would be better," remarked the border ranchman, "if it had some lemon in it."

"Tomás," he said again, after expressing his thanks, "I want you to tell us why you left Mexico to come to Texas."

"A coyote," the goat-herder dallied, "has killed a black kid. It has always been known that coyotes will not molest a goat that is black. Something strange is waiting to happen. Perhaps it will snow this winter."

But at last Tomás got his tale going. This is what he told.

Deep within the Sierra Madre, in the state of Chihuahua, on what is known as the Arroyo Colorado, Tomás as a young man lived and worked for a merchant named Joaquin Villareal. The store was the only store of the village — a mere agroupment of huts. Around it were great forests running down into the canyons and crawling up to the mountain crests. Scattered back

Not the Will of God

in the mountains lived a few timber cutters, and they all depended upon Don Joaquin Villareal. He furnished them what scanty supplies they had and periodically went out to check the ties they had cut. Then, maybe once a year, they came into the village and settled their accounts.

Once when the time came to make a checking of the ties, Don Joaquin took sick. He decided to send Tomás in his place. Tomás knew all the men and he knew the country in a general way, though he had never made one of these trips of inspection.

He must, he knew, go prepared with bed and provisions. So with a canteen of water on one side of his flat-horned saddle, a morral (a fiber bag) of frijoles and tortillas on the other, and a blanket tied on behind, he set forth.

"My mule," admonished Don Joaquin, "will show you the way."

She was a good little mule, but Tomás's trouble was that he did not take enough provisions. He had forgotten how large and sparsely settled the country was. At the end of four days he had checked two tie-cutters and had consumed all his food but a half-dozen buttons of garlic and that many tortillas. That evening he came to a poor, lonely *jacal*, or cabin. He recognized the inhabitant who came out to meet him as one of his employer's men named Ignacio. He was hospitably invited in to eat and spend the night.

"Though we have very little," said Ignacio, "it is yours."

Little enough it proved. For supper there was nothing but parched corn and tea from mulato bark without sugar. Tomás went out to his saddle, took from the morral the garlic and six tortillas he had left, and added them to the table. It was a feast for the tie-cutter and his wife. They appeared to have no children.

After they were through eating, Tomás said, "Tell me why you live so hard, this way."

Ignacio replied: "We have always lived hard this way. It is the will of God that we should always live this way."

There was silence for a long time. Then the woman said: "No, it is not the will of God. We could have had plenty, but my husband has not willed it."

"How is that?" asked Tomás.

"I will tell you. It is nearly ten years ago now — ten years next Christmas. It was cold. In the late evening an old, old Indian came to our *jacal*. His blanket was but shreds. The sandals on his feet were worn through. We gave him such food as we had. We had some wild artichokes as well as parched corn. The Indian was grateful. He told us a strange, strange story.

Not the Will of God

"He said that he was the very last of his tribe. I do not remember their name, but when I was a child I heard my grandmother's mother tell of their fierceness. From the earliest times this tribe had warred against the Government. The Government had forced them back into the wildest parts of the mountains. Here for years they existed but to get revenge. They got revenge by raiding every pack train that passed. In those days, you know, the Spaniards had wonderful mines at Tayopa, Gloria Pan, and other places in the Sierra Madre and brought gold and silver out on pack mules.

"The Indians killed the guards. They captured bullion of silver and bars of gold. They captured jewels meant for cathedrals and for daughters of the rich. They captured guns and ammunition and saddles plated with silver. They captured also a great bronze image of a man. All this stuff they put in a cave.

"This cave, so the old Indian said, was a room twenty feet wide and thirty feet long. First one entered a cavern without limits. Then one went through a narrow passage. Then one was in the treasure chamber. The Indians had no desire for wealth. All they desired was their old freedom. They did not want the Spaniards ever to recover the riches. In time the pack trains ceased to pass. The rich mines were closed.

"Then the Indians sealed up the passage between the

[333]

big cavern and the room full of riches. At one place, though, they left the wall very thin. In front of this false wall they set a kind of trap. Behind it they placed the image of the bronze man, and in his hand they fixed a sharp, strong dagger. Should anyone step on the trap, the bronze man would lunge through the false wall and tilt forward so as to stab the intruder to the heart.

"The entrance to the big cavern was naturally well hidden by some boulders. The Indians hid it even better. They had an understanding that the treasure should never be taken from the cave except in the presence of all members of the tribe.

" 'And now,' the old Indian said as he finished telling us all this, 'I am the last of the tribe. The others are all dead; most of them were killed. I can unlock the door. I have the right to dispose of the wealth. You have been generous to me, but it is plain that you live very hard. Why?'

"Then my husband Ignacio answered, 'Because God wills it.'

" 'No,' replied the Indian, 'God no longer wills thus. Come with me and I will give you and your wife enough to let you live in plenty all the rest of your life.'

"The next morning very early my husband Ignacio left. The Indian waited here near the *jacal* all day. Ignacio did not return until long after dark. The Indian had left while the sun was setting. He was gone one year exactly. He came again on Christmas day. Again we gave him warmth and such food as we had. He was grateful. Again he asked why we continued to live so hard, and once more Ignacio replied that it was the will of God.

"The Indian then repeated his whole story. I know it was true, for he told it exactly as he told it the first time. 'Come with me in the morning,' he said to Ignacio, 'and I will take you to where there is a great plenty.'

"Early next morning before daylight Ignacio went away. I gave the Indian some breakfast. He asked me where my husband had gone. I did not know. He asked me when he would return. I did not know. He waited many hours, waited for Ignacio to return so that he might lead him to the cave of riches. He said it was not more than a day on foot, on into the mountains. At sunset, when he saw that Ignacio would not return so long as he remained, the Indian went away. He has never been back.

"No, it is not the will of God that we live thus on parched corn. It is the will of Ignacio."

After Tomás heard this account he slept and then rode on to inspect the ties cut by other men. When he got back to the village, he told his employer, Don Joaquin Villareal, what he had heard.

Apache Gold and Yaqui Silver

Don Joaquin, who had recovered from his illness, at once determined to search for the cave. He went to Chihuahua City and secured a permit to prospect for mines. He took Tomás with him and an extra mule with provisions. They went to Ignacio's *jacal*, and then they traveled west, deeper into the mountains. After they had been looking a long, long time, they spied a hole in the top of a mountain. They threw rocks down the hole. They had to wait many seconds before they heard the rocks hit and echo below. The echoing sounds told them there was a cavern beneath.

Don Joaquin thought it best to enter the cavern through a tunnel from one side. A deep ravine cutting down one side of the mountain afforded a practicable place at which to start the tunnel. From a *ranchería* not far off and from other places Don Joaquin hired about twenty men, established a good camp, and set about his great work.

There was nothing but rock, rock, rock. The laborers cut their way into it by inches, carrying the chipped pieces out in *zurrones* — rawhide bags slung from the head of the carriers. They worked until Don Ignacio's funds for hiring men were exhausted. Then the only way he could keep on after the treasure was to promise each laborer a share of what he knew would eventually be found. At the end of six months they struck a kind of reddish sandstone that appeared to have been wet with blood. Quickly they tunneled through it and were in an enormous cavern.

The cavern was empty. Yet some animal bones and many marks of fire showed that human beings had once been there and had eaten. Far, far overhead could be seen a speck of light, through the discovery hole. But the cavern was dark, the light that came through the long tunnel being almost as dim as that from the hole overhead. All exploring had to be done with candles. The emptiness and the darkness discouraged the workmen, and now all but four of them quit. One of the four who remained was Tomás. Don Joaquin was not discouraged.

For days he went about the walls of the cavern, striking into them with a pick, Tomás holding the light. Tallow was costly, and they had to use sotol stalks for torches. Finally Don Joaquin struck a piece of wall that sounded hollow. Then with a few strokes he broke through.

In the dim light made by the torch of sotol stalk, which could hardly penetrate the dust, Tomás and Don Joaquin saw in front of them a figure of bronze larger than a real man. In its right hand was a dagger, securely bound there by rawhide thongs. Perhaps the trap-door had not been correctly built; perhaps many years of standing had caused it to grow stiff. Anyway, God was good and the dagger did not lunge forward to stab the intruders.

Tomás and his master were in the treasure room. The old Indian had told the truth. There were piles of silver bars, of gold, jewels, guns, silver-mounted saddles, finely wrought bridles, finely engraved swords.

The discovery was made close to dark on a Saturday. Don Joaquin said: "We are tired almost to death. Work and hunger have made us weak. Wealth so sudden has made us weaker. Let us rest tomorrow, the day of God, and give thanks to Him. On Monday morning we five shall divide all things. Any man who wishes may go to the village, but not a word must be said of this discovery. I and one other of you will sleep in the entrance to the tunnel so that no stranger shall enter."

Only two of the laborers went to the village. They drank much tequila and they talked. A large guard of soldiers on their way to fight the Yaqui Indians were camped in this village. Some of the officers heard the talk of the miners.

About daylight on Monday morning, Don Joaquin's camp was surprised and he and all his men were made prisoners. Also, other men who had helped with the work but who had deserted were brought in as prisoners. Then, chained together, the captives were marched

southward. They left the wild mountains and came into a country that had cart roads. They were fed almost nothing. They were jabbed and beaten when they lagged. Some of them died.

Finally, after having been driven for weeks over hundreds of miles, the remnant of prisoners were cast into a dark prison of thick rock walls. Tomás had a cell into which no light at all entered. Tortillas and water were brought to him by a guard carrying a lantern. The guard always left immediately and he ate in darkness.

He stayed there until he lost all account of time and the seasons.

Then, without explanation, he was liberated. He did not know why he had been made prisoner; he did not know why he had been freed. He made his way north to the village in the Sierra Madre. There he learned how Don Joaquin had been stood against a 'dobe wall and shot. The village was all but deserted. An old man said that tie-cutters no longer worked in the forests. Tomás came on north and crossed the Rio Grande.

"Señores," he concluded his tale, "I have told you the truth. These eyes have seen all that I have described. These hands held the pick that dug and they held the sotol stalk that lighted up the man of bronze with a dagger in his hand and then the treasure. These feet walked with chains. That the army officers got the treasure I am sure. They may have left something. I do not know. At least the cavern with the tunnel into it is still there."

General Mexhuira's Ghost

GENERAL MEXHUIRA'S GHOST

Although it was a full hour after our leisurely break-fast when the *mozo* conducted Doctor Black and my-self into the enormous room, Slinger, straight out of the bed, met us in his pajamas. They were of the hue and texture of those blanket-sized red silk bandannas imported from the Orient, the design on them the quet-zalcoatl — the plumed serpent of the Aztecs; and as he moved the serpents seemed to writhe. Thus appareled, wearing sandals of brilliant blue straw, in his mouth a freshly-lighted black cigarette of opiate fumes, his scraggy eyebrows and tousled mass of hair snow-white, he appeared as bizarre as his surroundings. I could not for some time concentrate my observation on either, and I do not know yet which dominated the other.

The enormous room, as cold as an underground cell, without stove, gas or fireplace, a huge old brass brazier by the writing table appearing to serve merely as an-other antiquity, was lined with rawhide-bound books that had been branded by monks of Spanish times and with bales of manuscripts, some of them parchment, that had been gathered from abandoned sacristies and

[343]

uprooted *científico* libraries over half of Mexico. Some of the shelves were heaped with terra cotta heads and figures common to Aztec ruins; among them reposed stone gods of the same ancient people. Stone artifacts and figures cluttered the floor about the walls. One that drew my attention particularly was a jade-green stone shaped somewhat like a half-egg and carved with the ubiquitous quetzalcoatl. In this room Slinger slept and sometimes ate as well as read. As Doctor Black and I shivered in our overcoats — in wintertime any spot of Mexico City out of the sun is bitter cold — Slinger did not even bother to wrap himself in the Oaxaca blanket that lay ready on a chair beside his bed.

Something of an antiquarian by taste and a collector by virtue of the pack-rat instinct inherent in most men, he was a physician by profession and had spent thirty-five of his sixty-odd years practising in "the Republic." It was through Black, who had been in medical school with him, that I received the invitation to inspect his collection. In particular I wanted to examine a manuscript said to be four centuries old and to contain a description of certain tombs and bones of giants exhumed by conquistadores while digging for Aztec gold. I had heard of Doctor Slinger long before I saw him. I had heard how for years before her death he never allowed his wife to come into the room he occupied —

though the remainder of the house allowed her ample domain to wander through. I had heard people whose lives he had saved, so they said, swear by his skill and extol his kind heart. I had heard how at times he went off from a lucrative practice to live with Indians and absorb their herb lore. Members of the American colony in Mexico City generally had, it seemed, more opportunities to talk about him than to talk with him. Most of them agreed that he had become Mexicanized; upper Mexicans said that he was Indianized.

And now as I tried to take in the contents of the room, my eyes were arrested by a single photograph, framed in wood inlaid with bone, that sat on top of a cabinet. The eyes of the man in the photograph drew me towards them.

When I glanced at Doctor Slinger to make inquiry, his eyes were boring into me, but he waited for the question.

"Why, that is General Mexhuira," he answered.

"I never heard of him," I said.

"Quite possible," he replied, "but, for all that, he was the gamest general of the Revolution. He was the best friend I ever had. He died in my arms."

"Where was he from?"

"Why, from Oaxaca."

I knew that Slinger had practised in Oaxaca before

coming to Mexico City. It required little urging to learn more about General Mexhuira.

"He was in charge of the revolutionary forces of Oaxaca," Slinger went on. "Nobody else could have handled the Indians as he handled them. I was his chief surgeon. In fact, when the fighting was hottest I was his only surgeon. After one battle I, in twenty-four hours' time, operated on eight hundred men."

"But, Doctor Slinger," interposed his medical friend, "that sounds incredible, humanly impossible."

"Oh, I'll admit," Slinger laughed, "that some of the operations were hasty. A lot of the wounded would have died anyway. It was like administering extreme unction. I got so damned exhausted cutting and cutting that finally I had a *mozo* strap my body to his. He supported me and held me up while I went on using my arms to cut. I wouldn't have gone through what I did for anybody but Mexhuira.

"As everybody knows, when the Revolutionists finally won out, the country was still divided up among local leaders. Villa was still out in the north; to the west the followers of murdered Zapata remained unreconciled; the oil companies around Tampico were paying another general to protect them; and Mexhuira held out too. But the fighting was mostly over. There wasn't enough money left in Oaxaca to support a doctor, and I withdrew from the army and came up to Mexico City and opened the office I have now on the Avenida Cinco de Mayo. Everybody was watched in those days. For that matter, I am still watched. More than one Indian trying to smuggle a stone god or something like that in to me has been killed.

"Well, I had not been here long, when a government agent called on me to use my influence to persuade Mexhuira to give up. I thought it was the best thing for him to do. I received absolute promises that he would be safe physically, and then I went down to see him. He was a little fellow, weighing less than a hundred pounds. The force in a man's veins, the energy of his spirit, and the light in his eyes don't weigh, you know. He embraced me, trusted my judgment, and promised to come up to Mexico City right away and make his peace with the powers.

"He kept his promise. There was a whole corps of staff officers to meet him at the station; he was conducted to the President's palace, served a banquet, and then for two weeks wined and dined like a visiting king — which he was. I saw him nearly every day, and I saw him going to pieces. He never had been a city man; he was a man of the *campo*, a native of the wildest sierras. He was so aboriginal that when he started out he had the Mexican eagle on his flag clawing a plumed serpent instead of the rattlesnake. This quetzalcoatl reached clear across the flag. Some Indian had worked it into the cloth for Mexhuira. It was like a sign in the sky for drawing his followers, and he himself had such a belief in it that he would not have gone into battle without it.

"One afternoon I was summoned to the hospital, and there I found Mexhuira in a paroxysm of pain. He was absolute master of himself, however. He told me he had been poisoned, and after examining him I had no doubt of the fact. I don't go around publishing this opinion. Such suffering as his could not last. When his pain was at its worst, I held him in my arms as I would hold a child, and thus he died.

"I saw attendants lay him out, and then I came home and came into this room to read and try to throw off my depression of spirit. I had lost, as I have already told you, the best friend of my life. For maybe an hour I had been trying to read — and I always use strong lights — when I heard a slight noise. Looking up, I saw Mexhuira.

" 'What are you doing here?' I said.

" 'I have come to tell you good-by and to make a request,' he answered.

"He was standing in front of me and I reached out to grasp his hand. I could not feel it. Then I passed my hand through his body without feeling it. Yet he looked natural and his voice sounded natural.

General Mexhuira's Ghost

" 'No,' he said, 'you cannot feel my body. I am dead, nothing but a spirit. The request I make is this: that you educate my two sons and see that they get a square start in life; that you guard my daughter until she is married; and that you act as adviser to my wife. You will need money to fulfil such a guardianship.'

"Then he told me to go to a certain number on a certain street. There I was to knock. An Aztec Indian would appear. This I wondered at, for Mexhuira was himself a Mixteco. Anyway I was to give this Indian the password, a word in his tongue that you would not remember if I repeated it to you. 'Whatever money you require will be delivered to you,' Mexhuira said.

"I promised him on my soul to care for his wife and children. Then we talked for a long while about various matters. He told me that since dying he had learned the absolute facts about his poisoning, and he detailed the circumstances, not omitting names of politicians. A little before daybreak he said he must go. 'I have to be back with my body,' he explained. Then he came nearer and put his arms around me. Though I cannot swear that I felt them, I seemed to feel them. With a 'May God go with you,' he was gone.

"The newspapers had long accounts of the sudden death of General Mexhuira with the usual pictures of the corpse and with comments on his frail body. The

president expressed deep mourning and sent his condo-
lences both to Mexhuira's family and his native state.
After that he was buried with military pomp, as a
national hero, here in the nation's capital.

"I had a good practice and was kept busy. Now and
then I heard an echo of dissatisfaction from the south,
where the Indians, it seemed, wanted their Mexhuira
back. Then I read that the Government had decided to
take up the body and move it to Oaxaca. In all of this
I was not consulted. I am getting ahead of the order of
events, however.

"The day after I saw Mexhuira buried, I ordered my
chauffeur to drive me to the house where I was to get
the money. The street was so little known that we had
to go to police headquarters to learn its direction. It
proved to be away out on the edge of town. I knocked
at the number; it was over a closed door to a run-down
adobe building. A blanketed Indian opened — old, silent, erect. Though polite in his salutation, he looked
at me searchingly. I merely gave the password.

" 'How much do you want?' he asked.

" 'Five thousand in gold.'

" 'Does it have to be all in gold?'

" 'Yes,' I said, 'it needs to be all in gold.'

" 'Very well,' he said, 'come back at sunset and the
money will be ready for you.'

"I was back there at sunset. The old Indian invited me into his house. It was as bare as the usual Indian house. He closed the door. Then he delivered a heavy bag made of dressed pigskin.

" 'There is one other thing you are to have,' he said. With that he indicated a jade-looking rock carved with the plumed serpent and shaped something like a half-egg."

At these words my eyes turned to the stone I had already noticed.

"Yes, that is it," Slinger said.

"Slinger," Doctor Black broke in, "I did not know that you drank those mescal cocktails before breakfast."

"I don't," he answered vigorously. "You can smell my breath if you want to."

My companion not only smelt his breath but felt his pulse. He told me later that he could detect no evidence of alcohol.

"Go on," I said.

Slinger went on.

"The old Indian volunteered that the green rock had come out of the Buried City of Mexico — *La Ciudad Enterrada*. I suppose you have heard of it. All the natives in Mexico know about it, how it lies enchanted and how it holds more riches than Montezuma or Cortés ever dreamed of. The old Aztec knew somehow about my interest in antiquities, and he asked if I'd like to see the city. I did see it — but all that belongs at another place. I did not ask where the money came from. The Indian carried it and the stone to my car. I brought them both home, and at once began spending the money on Mexhuira's family.

"And now to get back to the removal of Mexhuira's body to Oaxaca. I read that there was to be a military escort. About twelve o'clock on the day that the body was to be conducted out of the city, I was performing a minor operation in a room adjoining my office. The window of this room, overlooking Avenida Cinco de Mayo, was open. A nurse was assisting me. I had just given the patient, a man, a local anesthetic when, all of a sudden, we all heard a blare of military music. Military bands and parades are far from uncommon in Mexico City, as you know, and it was only with a mild curiosity that I stepped to the window to look out.

"What was passing was the funeral cortège of General Mexhuira. The black coffin, draped with flags, was on a caisson. Then Mexhuira himself floated into the window. When he did, the nurse fainted and the man rolled off the operating table in a faint also. I am sure that I alone heard my friend's words.

" 'I know you were not expecting me,' he said, 'and I have only a minute to stay. They are taking me back home where I belong. There I'll be at rest. I have come to give the last farewell.' Then he thanked me for the way in which I was taking care of his family, told me again that when I needed money the old Indian would furnish it, gave me a final *abrazo*, and floated out of the window. I saw him float over the crowds in the street, rest a moment on the caisson, wave me an *adiós*, and disappear into the coffin. You may think it strange, and I thought it damned strange, that while the nurse and the man to be operated on should have seen him, no one in the street was aware of his presence. After a bit the nurse came to, and with her help I finished with the patient. I could have cut his liver out, he was so thoroughly unconscious.

"That was the last I ever saw of Mexhuira. His boys I kept for several years at a school in Texas. With a suitable education each of them now has an excellent position. The girl I kept in a private school here in Mexico City, and she is well married. She has begun having babies and won't have time from now on to be unhappy. The widow lived well provided for until last year, when she died.

"No, I never took a centavo from the old Aztec that I did not spend on the family. I'll be honest and say I knew Mexhuira, both alive and dead, too well to misuse any of the money.

[353]

Apache Gold and Yaqui Silver

"And now," Slinger concluded in his hearty voice, "we'll examine that material on the ancient giants of Mexico. I am sorry that the room seems cold. After a man has run with the Indians down here as much as I have, his nerves and senses go to recording stimuli in a different way."

"Before we take up the giants, Doctor Slinger," I said, trying to keep my teeth from chattering, "I wish you'd finish what you started to say about that green rock."

"Oh, yes, that rock. Well, when I went back to have the old Aztec guide me to the Buried City of Mexico, he made me swear all kinds of oaths of secrecy. And don't imagine for a minute that the watch kept over a man after he has sworn an Indian oath and been made partner to an Indian secret is just fiction stuff. I know. I was blindfolded — even if that's fiction stuff also. All I know about the course we took is that we went out of the Aztec's house by the back door, which opens into a big walled-in yard. He seemed to lead me down some kind of tunnel.

"When the blinds were taken off, we were on the edge of a street paved with cobblestones and lined with squat rock houses. The fronts of these houses were so becarved with plumed serpents and other figures of strange beasts and the light was pulsing in such a way that you might have imagined you were looking down on one of those conventions of rattlesnakes the Indians tell about. They say that sometimes hundreds and hundreds and thousands of snakes come writhing and crawling together, usually in some canyon, and there twist into a solid mass that keeps on twisting. Those plumed serpents on the houses and temples of the Buried City had been fixed there, in stone, for thousands of years; yet somehow the light made them seem to be moving. I could not for the life of me make out where the light came from. It actually looked as if it were coming out of the eyes of the snakes. I saw hundreds of jade stones the size and shape of this, carved in the same way. This is the only proof I have of what I tell you. I used to think I'd like to possess some of the riches of that *Ciudad Enterrada*, and reveal its existence, after all these centuries still only legendary, to the world. Maybe it's having become an Indian myself that has killed such ambitions dead, maybe it's the years."

At this juncture a servant brought up Doctor Slinger's breakfast, which he at once set about prefacing with mescal cocktails for the company as well as for himself.

"Maybe it's Mexhuira cocktails," Doctor Black added.

"They belong to the country," Slinger observed.

Apache Gold and Yaqui Silver

I did not learn a single fact from the manuscript about the giants of ancient Mexico. The Buried City of Enchantment never was supposed to be documented.

Appendix

as from air flights and air pilots. Langford Johnston's son, L. R. Johnston, Selma, California, sent me another manuscript embodying his father's story. I have singled out these four helpers for special mention, but about fifty other persons who talked or wrote to me have my thanks. Their fiber is in the pattern I have tried to weave. I want to list the whole generous crew.

Mr. and Mrs. C. A. Anderson, Kingston, New Mexico. Johnny Allred, Glenwood, New Mexico. S. D. Baldwin, Lordsburg, New Mexico. H. B. Birmingham, Horse Springs, New Mexico. Frank Childress, Paxson Springs (Grants), New Mexico. Morris Coates, Mogollon, New Mexico. Max M. Coleman, Lubbock, Texas. James H. Cook, Agate, Nebraska. Maurice Crain, New York, N. Y. Ruth Dodson, Mathis, Texas. R. S. Emmett: letter dated Mar. 5, 1882, to Sylvester Baxter, in office of Arizona State Historian, Phoenix, Arizona. George Fitzpatrick, Santa Fe, New Mexico. Herman Funk, Magdalena, New Mexico. J. Leeper Gay, Prescott, Arizona. James B. Gray, Albuquerque, New Mexico. I. E. Hanson, Lawton, Oklahoma. James D. Hill, Superior State Teachers College, Superior, Wisconsin. Alvin D. Hudson, El Paso, Texas. W. I. (Bill) Johnston, Magdalena, New Mexico, son of the famous searcher, Langford Johnston. Lee Jones, El Paso, Texas. Lewis Jones, Glenwood, New Mexico. Will Jones, Reserve, New Mexico. George Krause, Mogollon, New Mexico. Tom Lea, Sr., El Paso, Texas. Chalk Lewis, Agua Frio (Grants), New Mexico. R. W. (Bob) Lewis, Magdalena, New Mexico. Mrs. J. Lee Loveless, Chandler, Arizona. Charlie McCarty, Reserve, New Mexico. E. B. McIntosh, Las Cruces, New Mexico. Rose Anne Mason, West Los Angeles, California. Charles Newcomb, Baca, New Mexico. Charles M. Newman, El Paso, Texas. Lee Newman, El Paso, Texas. Mrs. John Payne, Tres Lagunas, New Mexico. F. Gerald Phillips, Albany, New York. Cole Railston, Magdalena, New Mexico. G. C. Robinson, Ramirena, Texas. Frank W. Seward, El Paso, Texas. Clem Smith, Lordsburg, New Mexico. Montague Stevens, Luna, New Mexico. Nat Straw, Cliff, New Mexico. Pat Sullivan, El Paso, Texas. C. W. L. Stevens, Los Angeles, California. A. M. Tenney, Jr., Fabens, Texas. A. M. Tenney, Sr., El Paso, Texas — and the Sierra Madre of Mexico. N. Howard (Jack) Thorp, Alameda, New Mexico. R. W. (Dick) Tighe, Magistral, Durango, Mexico. W. T. Tolbert (deceased), El Paso, Texas. Edith L. Watson, Denver, Colorado. R. A. Wheeler, Tucson, Arizona. Gordon W. Wilder, Caballo, New Mexico.

PRINTED SOURCES

(a) Books

McKenna, James A., Black Range Tales: Wilson-Erickson, Inc., New York, 1936.

Mitchell, John D., Lost Mines of the Great Southwest: The Journal Company, Inc., Phoenix, Arizona, 1933.

(b) Pamphlets

Allen, Charles, The Adams Diggings Story: Hughes-Buie Co., El Paso, Texas, 1935.

Byerts, W. H., Gold: The Adams Gold Diggings, n. p., 1919.

(c) Newspaper and Magazine Articles

Adventure magazine, 1922 (?): "Campfire" letters by Max M. Coleman, John L. Riggs, and L. V. Carothers;

Appendix

Nov. 30, 1923, "Ask Adventure" section; May 20, 1924, "Campfire" letter by Max M. Coleman.

Albuquerque (N. M.) *Daily Citizen*, Sept. 26 and Dec. 3, 1888. The Paterson Expedition.

Albuquerque (N. M.) *Tribune*, April 10 and 11, 1934: "Off the Beaten New Mexico Path," by George Fitzpatrick.

Arizona Daily Star, Tucson, Ariz., Nov. 11, 12, 13, 1924: "Turner's Own Story," as related to Frank Scully.

Arizona Enterprise (Phoenix), Jan. 28, 1890.

Arizona Republic, about 1936: "The Lost Adams Diggings," by Chas. M. Clark, Pres. Arizona Pioneers Ass'n.

Chandler (Ariz.) *Arizonan:* "Daring Prospectors Sacrifice Lives in Search of Old Mine," John D. Mitchell.

Deming, New Mexico, *Graphic*, Aug. 3–Oct. 25, 1927: A serial entitled "Lost Canyon Diggings," by "Uncle Jimmie" [James A. McKenna], later incorporated in McKenna's book *Black Range Tales*, New York, 1936.

El Paso, Texas, *Herald*, Feb. 19, 1916; reprinted Sept. —, 1921: "Lost Adams Diggin's," etc., by W. H. Byerts, of Socorro, N. M. With very little change the same material appeared in the pamphlet issued by Byerts in 1919. July 2, 1927: "Story of Rich Placer as Adams Related It; Others Have Sought It" – page feature; July 16, 1927: "Renegade Indians and White Outlaws Are Guarding Placer Even Today, Hudson Believes" – page feature; Aug. 6, 1927: "El Pasoan Tells How He Got Map to Hidden Placer" – page feature with pictures; Aug. 13, 1927: "Prospector Spends 40 Yrs. Hunting Lost Adams Diggin's" – Langford Johnston's story as told by Tolbert in interview, with map; Dec. 24, 31, 1927 and Jan. 7 and 14, 1928: Brewer account as related by A. M. Tenney, Jr.; May 7, 1928 and May 10, 1929: sketches by W. S. Hunter in his column "Around

Appendix

Here"; Aug. 5, 1929: "Renew Search for Fabled Gold Hoard"; Apr. 4, 1930: "El Paso School Janitor Certain He Can Find Old Lost Gold Mine."

El Paso (Texas) *Herald-Post,* Oct. 18, 1932: rehash of Byerts narrative by Marshall Hail; Sept. 21, 1937: "The Lost Adams Diggings Are Still Lost," by L. Bruce Hatfield, in "Thinking Out Loud" column.

Frontier Times, Bandera, Texas, April, 1928: "More about the Lost Adams Diggings," by Col. C. C. Smith, U. S. A. retired; Dec., 1934, "The Adams Diggings," by Chas. A. Gianini; Jan., 1935, "The Adams Diggings," by Max Coleman.

Grants, New Mexico — pamphlet issued by Chamber of Commerce, Grants, N. M., 1938.

Long Beach (Cal.) *Press Telegram,* 1931: "Harrowing Adventures of a Hunter of Buried Treasure," by Geo. A. England.

Mogollon Range, Mogollon, New Mexico, an annual issue of the 1920's.

New Mexico, Albuquerque, N. M., Sept., 1935: "Lost Mines and Buried Gold," by Eleanor Kay.

Overland Monthly, San Francisco, California, Feb., 1924: article on Adams Diggings by J. D. Hill.

Salt Lake Mining Review, Salt Lake City, Utah, June 15, 1925: "Adams and His Box Canyon Gold," by Jas. D. Hill.

Santa Fe (N. M.) *New Mexican,* June 11, 1929: "Secret of Old Adams Gold Diggin's Well Kept by Mother Earth" — an interview with Col. Jack Flemming taken from Silver City *Enterprise.*

Silver City (N. M.) *Enterprise,* Dec. 14, 1888: Patterson expedition.

Sportsman Pilot, The, Albany, N. Y., Nov., 1931: "It's

Appendix

Thar Aplenty for Them That Finds It," by F. Gerald Phillips.

Street and Smith's *Western Story Magazine*, May, 1933, and other issues undated.

Tucson (Arizona) *Citizen*, Apr. 26, 1929.

Washington (D. C.) *Star*, Sept. 23, 1899: Interview from Frederick W. Hodge on buried treasure and lost mines of the West.

Clippings unidentified. Several from New Mexico papers given me by Herman Funk of Magdalena.

II · A Note on Scalp Hunters in Mexico

I hope to see some day a full account of the scalp hunters of northern Mexico and their activities. The makings of a lusty book are here. As a contribution towards it, I set down such sources as I have come across.

Bancroft, H. H., *History of the North Mexican States and Texas*, II, 599–601; *History of Arizona and New Mexico*, 487–488.

Bobbit, E. B., Bvt. Major, Assistant Quartermaster, letter from, dated San Antonio, Oct. 15, 1849, filed under title of *Bureau of Indian Affairs Concerning Texas*, Vol. 3, University of Texas Archives. Extract of the letter follows: "A party of Americans has engaged in the service of the State of Chihuahua to kill and destroy Indians, for whose scalps they are to receive from $50 to $500, according to the official importance of the victim; these men have recently entered into our territory near the Presidio del Norte and killed and scalped a number of peaceable and friendly Indians — which has so exasperated the Indians along the whole frontier, that the life of every white man who may fall into their power must pay the cost — nothing short of a very general hostility on the part of the Indians against the whites is anticipated as the result of the shameful conduct of these degraded mercenaries who bear the name of Americans."

Bartlett, John R., *Personal Narrative of Explorations and Incidents*, N. Y., 1854, I, 322–323.

Appendix

Bell, Major Horace, *Reminiscences of a Ranger*, Los Angeles, 1881, 267–273.

Bourke, John G., *On the Border with Crook*, London, 1892, 73, 83, 84, 117–118.

Cady, John H., *Arizona's Yesterday*, n. p., 1915, 27.

Connelley, William Elsey, *Doniphan's Expedition*, Kansas City, Mo., 1907, 101–102, 327, 388–389, 400, 416–421. Connelley, whose work is a reprint of *Doniphan's Expedition* by John T. Hughes, with extended annotation and supplementation, indexes various minor references to Kirker, leader of the scalp hunters.

Dodge, Richard I., *Our Wild Indians*, Hartford, Conn., 1883, 245.

Edwards, Frank S., *A Campaign in New Mexico with Colonel Doniphan*, London, 1848, 62.

Edwards, M. B., diary of, included in *Marching with the Army of the West*, 1846–1848, edited by Ralph P. Bieber, Glendale, Calif., 1936, 237, 253.

Froebel, Julius, *Seven Years Travel in Central America, Northern Mexico, and the Far West*, London, 1859, 350–351, 354, 440–441, 528. Froebel is as circumstantial as Ruxton in picturing the Comanche and Apache terrorization of northern Mexico; see pp. 331–397.

Frontier Times, Bandera, Texas, Oct., 1926: article on Edward A. Weyman by Hunter Anderson.

Gibson, George R., *Journal of a Soldier*, ed. by Ralph P. Bieber, Glendale, Calif., 1935, 335. According to the editor's note, "In 1847 the *St. Louis Post* published a biographical sketch of James Kirker, which was copied by the *Santa Fe Republican*, Nov. 20, 1847."

Gregg, Josiah, *Commerce of the Prairies*, N. Y., 1844, as

Appendix

reprinted and edited by Thwaites, *Early Western Travels*, XX, 103.

Guajardo, Alberto A., Piedras Negras, Coahuila, Mexico: documents of northern Coahuila in possession of.

Hobbs, Captain James, *Wild Life in the Far West*, Hartford, 1872, 71–100, 111–112, 409.

Kendall, George Wilkins, *Narrative of the Texan Santa Fe Expedition*, N. Y., 1847, II, 56–62.

Lane, Walter P., *The Adventures and Recollections of*, Marshall, Texas, 1887, 48–52. The "John Glandon" here treated of was John Glanton.

Newcomb, James P., *Sketch of Secession Times in Texas and Journal of Travel from Texas through Mexico to California, including a History of the "Box Collony,"* San Francisco, California, August, 1883, 21–23 (in Part II).

Ober, F. A., *Travels in Mexico*, Boston, 1884, 627. Ober and other writers refer to the *Proyecta de Guerra*, 1837. A copy of this is said to be in the Wagner Collection, California, but I have not investigated.

Reid, Captain Mayne, *The Scalp Hunters*, N. Y., 1863. A historical novel.

Ruxton, George F., *Adventures in Mexico*, London, 1847, 151–156. Ruxton has left the most vivid account extant of Indian rapine in northern Mexico.

Sage, Rufus B., *Rocky Mountain Life*, Boston, 1858, 231, 355.

Santleben, August, *A Texas Pioneer*, N. Y., 1910, 165–166.

Wislizenus, A., *Memoir of a Tour to Northern Mexico*, 30th Congress, 1st Session, Senate Miscellaneous Documents, No. 26, Washington, 1848, 28.

Appendix

White, Owen P., *Out of the Desert*, El Paso, Texas, 1923, 29–30, 35.

Wilson, Benjamin Davis, *Observations on Early Days in California and New Mexico*, as dictated to Thomas Savage, 1877, 1–8, 44. Photostat of manuscript in Bancroft Library, Huntington Library, San Marino, California.